AICPA EDITORIAL STATEMENT TO READERS

The Personal Financial Planning Division of the American Institute of Certified Public Accountants (AICPA) has served as the technical editor for **"Prudent Practices for Investment Advisors (U.S. Edition)"** handbook. The AICPA's participation in the development of the handbook is intended to promote and protect the interests of the consumer public and to perpetuate the delivery of competent and objective investment advice.

This handbook was developed specifically for Investment Advisors – those who provide comprehensive and continuous investment advice including financial advisors, broker-consultants, investment consultants, wealth managers, financial consultants, trust officers, financial planners, and fiduciary advisers. This handbook will serve as a foundation for prudent investment fiduciary practices. It provides investment fiduciaries with an organized process for making informed and consistent decisions. Fiduciaries must, however, exercise professional judgment when applying the Practices; consulting legal counsel and other authorities when appropriate.

The investment practices contained within this handbook have been reviewed in detail by the Fiduciary Task Force of the AICPA's Personal Financial Planning Executive Committee. The full Executive Committee has reviewed the work of the Task Force and approves their conclusions. Even with this level of review, this handbook does not represent authoritative literature for CPAs practicing as a financial advisor. The AICPA's participation is solely in the capacity of technical editor.

Although the fiduciary practices primarily focus on many of the legal requirements of investment fiduciaries, the scope of the Handbook addresses the Employee Retirement Income Securities Act (ERISA), the Uniform Prudent Investor Act (UPIA), and the Uniform Management of Public Employee Retirement Systems Act (MPERS). Investment Advisors must become familiar, and comply, with all other federal and state laws applicable to the fiduciary's particular field of practice including the rules and restrictions imposed by regulatory bodies such as the Securities and Exchange Commission, General Accounting Office, Department of Labor/ERISA and the Internal Revenue Service.

We gratefully acknowledge the invaluable contributions of the many CPA's who were instrumental in the review of the Handbook. The PFP Division would also like to acknowledge the special efforts of Clark M. Blackman II, CPA/PFS, Ken A. Dodson, CPA/PFS, Joel Framson, CPA/PFS, Charles R. Kowal, JD, CPA, Michele L. Schaff, CPA/PFS, AIFA, and Scott K. Sprinkle, CPA/PFS.

The AICPA is the national professional organization of CPAs, with more than 330,000 members in business and industry, public practice, government, and education. For more information about the AICPA, visit its Web site at *www.aicpa.org*.

TABLE OF CONTENTS

PRACTICES AND PROCEDURES THAT DEFINE AN ADVISOR'S GLOBAL FIDUCIARY STANDARD OF EXCELLENCE

Introduction

Distribution Partners	6
It's About Process	7
It's About Excellence	9
It's About the Law	11
It's About the "Tone at the Top"	13
It's About the Benefits of Having a Defined Global Standard of Excellence	14
Legal Counsel's Editorial Statement	15
Comments to the UPIA, UPMIFA, and MPERS	16

Step 1: Organize

Practice A-1.1

The Advisor demonstrates an awareness of fiduciary duties and responsibilities. — 17

Practice A-1.2

Investments are managed in accordance with applicable laws, trust documents, and written investment policy statements (IPS). — 19

Practice A-1.3

The roles and responsibilities of all involved parties (fiduciaries and non-fiduciaries) are defined, documented, and acknowledged. — 21

Practice A-1.4

The Investment Advisor is not involved in self-dealing and has policies and procedures to address self-dealing of co-fiduciaries. — 22

Practice A-1.5

Service agreements and contracts are in writing, and do not contain provisions that conflict with fiduciary standards of care. — 24

Practice A-1.6

Assets are within the jurisdiction of appropriate courts, and are protected from theft and embezzlement. — 25

Step 2: Formalize

Practice A-2.1

An investment time horizon has been identified for each client. — 26

Practice A-2.2

A risk level has been identified for each client. — 28

Practice A-2.3

An expected, modeled return to meet investment objectives has been identified. — 30

Practice A-2.4

Selected asset classes are consistent with the risk, return, and time horizon. — 32

Practice A-2.5

Selected asset classes are consistent with implementation and monitoring constraints. — 33

TABLE OF CONTENTS

PRACTICES AND PROCEDURES THAT DEFINE AN ADVISOR'S GLOBAL FIDUCIARY STANDARD OF EXCELLENCE

Practice A-2.6
There is an IPS which contains the detail to define, implement, and monitor the client's investment strategy. 35

Practice A-2.7
The IPS defines appropriately structured, socially responsible investment (SRI) strategies (where applicable). 38

Step 3: Implement

Practice A-3.1
Each client's investment strategy is implemented in compliance with the required level of prudence. 41

Practice A-3.2
When safe harbors are elected, each client's investment strategy is implemented in compliance with the applicable provisions. 44

Practice A-3.3
Investment vehicles are appropriate for the portfolio size. 48

Practice A-3.4
A due diligence process is followed in selecting service providers, including the custodian. 51

Step 4: Monitor

Practice A-4.1
Periodic reports compare investment performance against an appropriate index, peer group, and IPS objectives. 52

Practice A-4.2
Periodic reviews are made of qualitative and/or organizational changes of investment decision-makers. 54

Practice A-4.3
Control procedures are in place to periodically review policies for best execution, "soft dollars," and proxy voting. 57

Practice A-4.4
Fees for investment management are consistent with agreements and with all applicable laws. 59

Practice A-4.5
"Finder's fees" or other forms of compensation that may have been paid for asset placement are appropriately applied, utilized, and documented. 61

Practice A-4.6
There is a process to periodically review the organization's effectiveness in meeting its fiduciary responsibilities. 63

Conclusion 65

Appendix A: Sample IPS 66

Glossary of Terms 77

INTRODUCTION

PRUDENT PRACTICES FOR INVESTMENT ADVISORS
(U.S. EDITION)

This publication is part of a series of fiduciary handbooks published by fi360 to define Global Standards of Excellence for investment fiduciaries. The handbooks are designed to be reference guides for knowledgeable investors, as opposed to in-depth "how to" manuals for persons who are not familiar with basic investment management procedures. Handbooks are available through fi360 (fi360.com) or through any of the Distribution Partners listed on the next page

Handbooks that are referenced as a "U.S. Edition" are fully substantiated by U.S. legislation, case law, and regulatory opinion letters. Handbooks that are referenced as a "Worldwide Edition" are substantiated by industry best practices.

Prudent Practices for Investment Stewards
(U.S. Edition)

Fiduciary practices for persons who have the legal responsibility for managing investment decisions (trustees and investment committee members).

Prudent Practices for Investment Advisors (U.S. Edition)

Fiduciary practices for professionals who provide comprehensive and continuous investment advice, including wealth managers, financial advisors, trust officers, investment consultants, financial consultants, financial planners, and fiduciary advisers.

Legal Memoranda (U.S. Edition)

Legal opinions and substantiation for all of the practices defined for Investment Stewards and Investment Advisors in the U.S.

Prudent Practices for Investment Stewards and Investment Advisors *(Worldwide Edition)*

Fiduciary practices which define a Global Standard of Excellence for Investment Stewards and Investment Advisors.

Fi360 has also developed handbooks and substantiation for Canada, New Zealand, and Singapore.

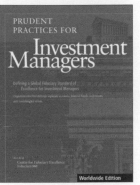

Prudent Practices for Investment Managers
(Worldwide Edition)

Fiduciary practices which define a Global Standard of Excellence for Investment Managers – professionals who have discretion to select specific securities for separate accounts, mutual funds, commingled trusts, and unit trusts.

Fi360 is also a founding member of **CEFEX** (Centre for Fiduciary Excellence), which is a global initiative established to define and promote Global Fiduciary Standards of Excellence, and to serve as an independent rating and certification organization.

CEFEX *has chosen the stylized version of the Greek letter "Phi," to represent fiduciary "trustworthiness" and/or "excellence."*

As a certifying organization, **CEFEX** also defines formal procedures to assess whether an investment fiduciary is in conformance with defined practices. An entry level verification is a first-party assessment, referred to as a SAFE™ (Self-Assessment of Fiduciary Excellence). A corresponding SAFE has been created for each handbook in the fiduciary series.

DISTRIBUTION PARTNERS

The following organizations serve as distributors for the fiduciary handbooks and SAFEs.

Actium, LLC	www.myactium.com
Alpha Wealth Strategies	www.alphawealthstrategies.com
American Portfolios	www.americanportfolios.com
Ardor Fiduciary Services, Ltd.	www.prudentfiduciary.com
Bruton Financial Advisors, LLC	www.brutonfinancial.com
BST Retirement Services, LLP	www.bstco.com
Canon Capital	www.canoncapital.com
Charles Schwab & Co., Inc.	www.schwab.com
Charles Stephen & Co., Inc.	www.charlesstephen.com
Chubb Group	www.chubb.com
Comerica, Inc.	www.comerica.com
Cornerstone Advisors Asset Management, Inc.	www.cornerstone-companies.com
Delaware Investments	www.delawareinvestments.com
Deutsche Bank	www.db.com
Federated Investors	www.federatedinvestors.com
Fidelity Investments	www.fidelity.com
Freund & Co. Investment Advisors, L.C.	St. Louis, MO
Gartmore Global Investments	www.gartmore.us
Ingham Group	www.ingham.com
Inspired Capitalworks	www.inspiredcapitalworks.com
Lindner Capital Advisors	www.lcaus.com
Managed Accounts Consulting Group of Prudential Investors	www.managedaccounts.com
Managers Investment Group	www.managersinvest.com
McKinley Investment Group, Inc.	www.mckinleyadvisors.com
Midwest Fiduciary	www.midwestfiduciary.com
National Association of College and University Business Officers (NACUBO)	www.nacubo.org
Plante Moran Financial Advisers	www.pmfa.com
Shea, Harley & Anderson	
Sheridan Road Financial	www.sheridanroad.com
Silver Oak Wealth Advisors, LLC	www.silveroakwa.com
Sprinkle Financial Consultants, LLC	Scott@sprinklefinancial.com
Stanton Group	www.stanton-group.com
Thornburg Investment Management	www.thornburginvestments.com
Victory Asset Management Co., Inc.	www.victoryasset.com
Wharton Advisors	www.whartonadvisors.net

IT'S ABOUT PROCESS

"Given the examination findings, we conclude that consultants should enhance their compliance policies and procedures to include those policies and procedures that will ensure that the adviser is fulfilling its fiduciary obligations to its advisory clients."

SEC's "STAFF REPORT CONCERNING EXAMINATIONS OF
SELECT PENSION CONSULTANTS" (MAY 16, 2005)

The vast majority of the world's liquid investable wealth is in the hands of investment fiduciaries, and the success or failure of investment fiduciaries can have a material impact on the fiscal health of any country. As critical as their role is, more has to be done to define the details of a fiduciary's prudent investment process.

This handbook is about the Practices a fiduciary should follow to demonstrate prudence in managing investment decisions. By following a structured process based on these Practices, the fiduciary can be confident that critical components of an investment strategy are being properly implemented.

The term, "fiduciary," can be divided further into three groups:

Investment Steward – *A person who has the legal responsibility for managing investment decisions (trustees and investment committee members).*

Investment Advisor – *A professional who is responsible for managing comprehensive and continuous investment decisions (including wealth managers, financial advisors, trust officers, financial consultants, investment consultants, financial planners, and fiduciary advisers).*

Investment Manager – *A professional who has discretion to select specific securities for separate accounts, mutual funds, commingled trusts, and unit trusts.*

This handbook is specifically written to define a Global Fiduciary Standard of Excellence for **Investment Advisors.**

Editorial Note: This document uses the terms "adviser" and "advisor."

"Adviser," as in "fiduciary adviser," is in reference to the term defined by the 2006 Pension Protection Act.

"Advisor," as used by fi360 throughout its materials, refers to the professional who is providing comprehensive and continuous investment advice.

Investment Advisors everywhere are looking for universally accepted standards of practice to aid them in the performance of their duties. Adherence to a standard can be the foundation for the trust placed in them by their clients, whether they are individuals or large organizations. Standards of excellence offer a consistency of interpretation and implementation, which facilitates the transfer of knowledge between the Advisor, clients, vendors, and regulators.

INTRODUCTION

IT'S ABOUT PROCESS

The legal and practical scrutinies Investment Advisors endure are tremendous, and come from multiple directions and for various reasons. Complaints and/or lawsuits alleging fiduciary misconduct are likely to increase. However, contrary to widespread belief, fiduciary liability is not determined by investment performance, but by whether a prudent process was followed. *It's not whether you win or lose; it's how you play the game.*

Oftentimes a fiduciary will confuse *responsibility* with *liability*. An Investment Advisor can never delegate away responsibility—it can be shared with other "co-fiduciaries," such as Investment Managers, but can never be fully discharged. However, the Investment Advisor can substantially mitigate the risk of liability by following prudent investment practices.

Similarly, investment products and techniques are never inherently imprudent. The way they are used and how decisions as to their use are made determines whether the prudence standard has been met. While even the most aggressive and unconventional investment can meet the standard if arrived at through a sound process, the most conservative and traditional one may be inadequate if a sound process was not implemented.

The key benefits of applying the Practices and procedures covered in this handbook include:

1. *Risk Management:* Most investment litigation involves the omission of certain fiduciary practices and/or prudent investment procedures, as opposed to the commission of certain acts. The handbook incorporates a "checklist" process to help the Investment Advisor ensure that investment decisions are prudently managed.

2. *Competitive Advantage:* "Fiduciary responsibility" has become the watchword with trustees, investment committee members, and even retail investors. Investment Advisors who can communicate clearly how they manage investment decisions to a defined fiduciary standard of excellence may enjoy a major advantage over competitors.

3. *Distinction as a Fiduciary Specialist:* More than eighty percent of the nation's liquid, investable wealth is managed by trustees and investment committees. Investment Advisors who desire to be at the top of their profession should be able to demonstrate fiduciary skills, knowledge, and responsibility in order to attract and retain key clients.

IT'S ABOUT EXCELLENCE

This handbook defines a Global Fiduciary Standard of Excellence for Investment Advisors. The scope of the "standard" is established by *"Practices,"* which are intended to provide the foundation and framework for a disciplined investment process.

The *Practices* are organized under a four-step Investment Management Process. The steps are consistent with the global ISO 9000 Quality Management System standard, which emphasizes continual improvement to a decision-making process:

Step 1: Organize

(Practices that begin with A-1.__)

Step 2: Formalize

(Practices that begin with A-2.__)

Step 3: Implement

(Practices that begin with A-3.__)

Step 4: Monitor

(Practices that begin with A-4.__)

For each *Practice*, one or more *Criteria* are provided to establish the scope of the *Practice*, and to help define the details of the standard of excellence.

A Suggested Procedure is provided with certain Practices to demonstrate how the *Practice* could be implemented. The Suggested Procedures are just that, suggestions on how we would implement a particular *Practice* if we were an Investment Advisor.

Fiduciary Quality Management System

(Analogous to the ISO 9000 QMS Continual Improvement Process)

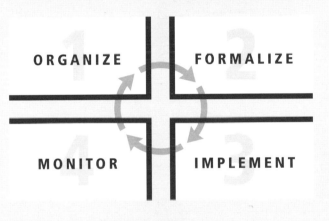

ORGANIZE   FORMALIZE

MONITOR   IMPLEMENT

Components of a Standard of Excellence

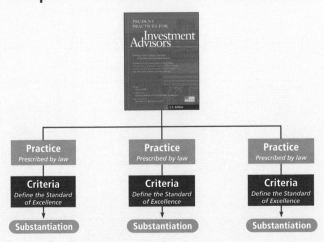

INTRODUCTION

IT's ABOUT EXCELLENCE

The twenty-three *Practices* for Investment Advisors are a mirror image of the *Practices* that have been defined for Investment Stewards, since one of the primary roles of the Advisor is to assist with the management of the Steward's fiduciary roles and responsibilities.

Investment Managers, on the other hand, have a unique role and an additional twenty-four *Practices* have been defined for evaluating whether an Investment Manager is worthy of a fiduciary mandate.

In total, forty-six different fiduciary *Practices* have been identified, detailing a prudent process for Investment Stewards, Investment Advisors, and Investment Managers. These Practices are summarized in *"The Periodic Table of Global Fiduciary Practices,"* copied below, but can be viewed in more detail in the foldout in the back of the handbook.

The Periodic Table of Global Fiduciary Practices

ORGANIZE (1)

Practice M-1.1 — Senior management demonstrates expertise in their field, and there is a clear succession plan in place.	**Practice M-1.2** — There are clear lines of authority and accountability, and the mission, operations, and resources operate in a coherent manner.		
Practice M-1.3 — The organization has the capacity to service its client base.	**Practice M-1.4** — Administrative operations are structured to provide accurate and timely support services and are conducted in an independent manner.	**Practice SA-1.1** — Investments are managed in accordance with applicable laws, trust documents, and written investment policy statements (IPS).	**Practice SA-1.2** — The roles and responsibilities of all involved parties (fiduciaries and non-fiduciaries) are defined, documented, and acknowledged.
Practice M-1.5 — Information systems and technology are sufficient to support administration, trading, and risk management needs.	**Practice M-1.6** — The organization has developed programs to attract, retain, and motivate key employees.	**Practice SA-1.3** — Fiduciaries and parties in interest are not involved in self-dealing.	**Practice SA-1.4** — Service agreements and contracts are in writing, and do not contain provisions that conflict with fiduciary standards of care.
	Practice M-1.7 — There is a formal structure supporting effective compliance.	**Practice SA-1.5** — Assets are within the jurisdiction of courts, and are protected from theft and embezzlement.	**ORGANIZE 1**

FORMALIZE (2)

Practice SA-2.1 — An investment time horizon has been identified.	**Practice SA-2.2** — A risk level has been identified.	**Practice M-2.1** — The organization provides disclosures which demonstrate there are adequate resources to sustain operations.	**Practice M-2.2** — The organization has a defined business strategy which supports their competitive positioning.
Practice SA-2.3 — An expected, modeled return to meet investment objectives has been identified.	**Practice SA-2.4** — Selected asset classes are consistent with the identified risk, return, and time horizon.	**Practice M-2.3** — There is an effective process for allocating and managing both internal and external resources and vendors.	**Practice M-2.4** — There are effective and appropriate external management controls.
Practice SA-2.5 — Selected asset classes are consistent with implementation and monitoring constraints.	**Practice SA-2.6** — There is an IPS which contains the detail to define, implement, and manage a specific investment strategy.	**Practice M-2.5** — The organization has a defined process to control its flow of funds and asset variation.	**Practice M-2.6** — Remuneration of the company and compensation of key decision-makers is aligned with client interests.
FORMALIZE 2	**Practice SA-2.7** — The IPS defines appropriately structured, socially responsible investment (SRI) strategies (where applicable).	**Practice M-2.7** — The organization has responsible and ethical reporting, marketing, and sales practices.	**Practice M-2.8** — There is an effective risk-management process to evaluate both the organization's business and investment risk.

MONITOR (4)

Practice M-4.1 — There is a defined process for the attribution and reporting of costs, performance, and risk.	**Practice M-4.2** — All aspects of the investment system are monitored and are consistent with assigned mandates.	**Practice SA-4.1** — Periodic reports compare investment performance against appropriate index, peer group, and IPS objectives.	**MONITOR 4**
Practice M-4.3 — Control procedures are in place to periodically review policies for best execution, "soft dollars," and proxy voting.	**Practice M-4.4** — There is a process to periodically review the organization's effectiveness in meeting its fiduciary responsibilities.	**Practice SA-4.2** — Periodic reviews are made of qualitative and/or organizational changes of investment decision-makers.	**Practice SA-4.3** — Control procedures are in place to periodically review policies for best execution, "soft dollars," and proxy voting.
		Practice SA-4.4 — Fees for investment management are consistent with agreements and with all applicable laws.	**Practice SA-4.5** — "Finder's fees" or other forms of compensation that may have been paid for asset placement are appropriately applied, utilized, and documented.
			Practice SA-4.6 — There is a process to periodically review the organization's effectiveness in meeting its fiduciary responsibilities.

IMPLEMENT (3)

Practice SA-3.1 — The investment strategy is implemented in compliance with the required level of prudence.	**IMPLEMENT 3**	**Practice M-3.1** — The asset management team operates in a sustainable, balanced, and cohesive manner.	**Practice M-3.2** — The investment system is defined, focused, and consistently adds value.
Practice SA-3.2 — The fiduciary is following applicable "Safe Harbor" provisions (when elected).	**Practice SA-3.3** — Investment vehicles are appropriate for the portfolio size.	**Practice M-3.3** — The investment research process is defined, focused, and documented.	**Practice M-3.4** — The portfolio management process for each distinct strategy is clearly defined, focused, and documented.
Practice SA-3.4 — A due diligence process is followed in selecting service providers, including the custodian.		**Practice M-3.5** — The trade execution process is defined, focused, and documented.	

LEGEND:
Practices in gold that begin with an "SA" define a fiduciary standard of excellence for Investment Stewards and Investment Advisors, and are all substantiated by U.S. legislation, regulatory opinion letters, and case law.

"SA" Practices highlighted are best reviewed in conjunction with Investment Managers Practices.

Practices in maroon that begin with an "M" define a fiduciary standard of excellence for Investment Managers.

IT'S ABOUT THE LAW

The legal *Substantiation* for each Practice is also provided. All twenty-three Practices are substantiated by legislation, case law, and/or regulatory opinion letters from:

ERISA—Employee Retirement Income Security Act (impacts qualified retirement plans).

UPIA—Uniform Prudent Investor Act (impacts private trusts).

UPMIFA—Uniform Prudent Management of Institutional Funds Act (impacts foundations, endowments, and government sponsored charitable institutions).

MPERS—Uniform Management of Public Employee Retirement Systems Act (impacts state, county, and municipal retirement plans).

See Comments section on page 16 for more information regarding these legislative acts.

If an Investment Advisor read all of these Acts and identified the common fiduciary practices the Advisor would discover seven common practices. We have coined the term "Global Fiduciary Precepts" to denote these seven practices. They are:

1. **Know standards, laws, and trust provisions.**

2. **Diversify assets to specific risk/return profile of client.**

3. **Prepare investment policy statement.**

4. **Use "prudent experts" (for example, an Investment Manager) and document due diligence.**

5. **Control and account for investment expenses.**

6. **Monitor the activities of "prudent experts."**

7. **Avoid conflicts of interest and prohibited transactions.**

We suggest that the Investment Advisor utilize the seven Global Fiduciary Precepts, as they represent the best probing questions an Advisor could ask of a prospective client:

How was your portfolio's current asset allocation determined?

When was the last time you updated your IPS?

What type of due diligence was performed on the investment options that currently exist in your portfolio?

What type of periodic monitoring have you applied to your portfolio?

Do you understand all of the fees and expenses associated with the various components of your investment program?

INTRODUCTION

IT'S ABOUT THE LAW

Also, we suggest that anytime a client asks an investment question, the Advisor should map the question against the seven Uniform Fiduciary Practices. For example, if a client were to ask: "Should I invest in a hedge fund?" The Advisor should be thinking:

How would this impact the client's asset allocation?

Does the client's IPS provide for this type of investment strategy?

Do we have the in-house capability to select and monitor this type of investment option

Will the overall investment management fees for the client rise if we participate in this type of investment strategy?

It's About the "Tone at the Top"

"Much has been written about 'tone at the top,' the ethical standards that Boards and chief executives set, and its importance cannot be overestimated. Organizational behavior oftentimes mirrors the standards of integrity and fair dealing (i.e., avoidance of conflicts of interests, and self entitlements) exhibited by Board members and high ranking officials."

NAVIGANT REPORT TO SAN DIEGO CITY EMPLOYEE RETIREMENT SYSTEM,
DATED JANUARY, 2006

Investment Stewards, Investment Advisors and Investment Managers who do not foster and promote a culture of fiduciary responsibility are going to lack the sensitivity and awareness to identify the fiduciary breaches of others. When a fiduciary has its own conflicts of interests, then that fiduciary will be marginalized at best; corrupted at worst.

"Society depends upon professionals to provide reliable, fixed standards in situations where the facts are murky or the temptations too strong. Their principal contribution is an ability to bring sound judgment to bear on these situations. They represent the best a particular community is able to muster in response to new challenges."

DR. ROBERT KENNEDY,
UNIVERSITY OF ST. THOMAS

Investment fiduciaries are challenged by the need to foster a culture of fiduciary responsibility that is defined by reliable, fixed standards. The management of investment decisions is not an easy task, even for trained investment professionals; and a nearly impossible task for lay decision-makers who serve as trustees and investment committee members of retirement plans, foundations, endowments, and personal trusts. Since professional and lay decision-makers depend on an assortment of industry vendors for assistance in managing their diverse roles and responsibilities, it is important to foster and promote a culture of fiduciary responsibility with all involved parties.

IT'S ABOUT THE BENEFITS OF HAVING A DEFINED GLOBAL STANDARD OF EXCELLENCE

The twenty-three *Practices* are easily adaptable to all types of portfolios, regardless of size or intended use, and should:

- Help to establish evidence that the Advisor is following a prudent investment process.

- Serve as a practicum for all parties involved with investment decisions (Investment Stewards, Investment Managers, accountants, and attorneys), and provide an excellent educational outline of the duties and responsibilities of Investment Advisors.

- Potentially help increase long-term investment performance by identifying appropriate procedures for:
    - Diversifying the portfolio across multiple asset classes and peer groups
    - Evaluating investment management fees and expenses
    - Selecting Investment Managers
    - Terminating Investment Managers that no longer are appropriate

- Help uncover investment and/or procedural risks not previously identified, which may assist in prioritizing investment management projects.

- Encourage Advisors to compare their practices and procedures with those of their peers.

- Assist in establishing benchmarks to measure the progress of the Investment Advisor.

Legal Counsel's Editorial Statement

The fiduciary practices described in this handbook address many of the ethical and professional requirements of Investment Advisors. In addition, the Investment Advisor must become familiar, and comply, with all other laws applicable to the Advisor's particular field of practice.

This handbook is not intended to be used as a source of legal advice. The Investment Advisor should discuss the topics with legal counsel knowledgeable in this specific area of the law. References to laws, case laws, and regulatory opinion letters are provided merely as substantiation to the suggested practices. Nor is this handbook intended to represent specific investment advice.

The scope of this handbook will not include: (1) financial, actuarial, and/or recordkeeping issues; (2) valuations of closely held stock, limited partnerships, hard assets, insurance contracts, hedge funds, or blind investment pools; and/or (3) risk management issues such as the use of derivative and/or synthetic financial instruments.

COMMENTS REGARDING THE UPIA, UPMIFA, AND MPERS

The UPIA was released by the National Conference of Commissioners on Uniform State Laws in 1994, and subsequently approved by the American Bar Association and American Bankers Association. The UPIA serves as a default statute for private trusts. Ordinarily, the provisions of a private trust prevail. If a trust document is silent regarding a particular fiduciary duty, such as the duty to diversify, then the provisions of the UPIA apply.

State Adoptions:

Alabama	Maine	Oklahoma
Alaska	Massachusetts	Oregon
Arizona	Maryland	Pennsylvania
Arkansas	Michigan	Rhode Island
California	Minnesota	South Carolina
Colorado	Mississippi	South Dakota
Connecticut	Missouri	Tennessee
District of Columbia	Montana	Texas
Hawaii	Nebraska	U.S. Virgin Islands
Idaho	Nevada	Utah
Illinois	New Hampshire	Vermont
Indiana	New Jersey	Virginia
Iowa	New Mexico	Washington
Kansas	North Carolina	West Virginia
	North Dakota	Wisconsin
	Ohio	Wyoming

In the opinion of the authors, states that have an Act substantially similar to UPIA (as it pertains to defining an investment fiduciary standard of care) are: Delaware, Florida, Georgia, and New York.

If a particular state is not identified above, then the Advisor is advised to seek the opinion of qualified legal counsel on the fiduciary standard of care that is applicable to that particular state, and whether any of the fiduciary practices covered in this handbook are not applicable.

MPERS was released in 1997 by the NCCUSL and may impact state, county, and municipal retirement plans. To date, Maryland and Wyoming are the only states that have formally adopted the act.

In the opinion of the authors, South Carolina has adopted an act substantially similar to MPERS (as it pertains to defining an investment fiduciary standard of care).

UPMIFA was released in July 2006 by the NCCUSL. It is now available for consideration of adoption by state legislatures. It impacts foundations, endowments, and government-sponsored charitable organizations. It is replacing UMIFA, which has been adopted by 47 states and the District of Columbia. To date, 13 states have adopted the act, along with six more states, the District of Columbia, and the U.S. Virgin Islands all currently considering adoption.

Please visit www.nccusl.org for more information on uniform state laws.

Step 1: Organize

THE ADVISOR DEMONSTRATES AN AWARENESS OF FIDUCIARY DUTIES AND RESPONSIBILITIES.

A fiduciary is defined as someone acting in a position of trust on behalf of, or for the benefit of, another party. Fiduciary status is sometimes difficult to determine, but not in the case of registered Investment Advisors—they are generally considered fiduciaries.

Unfortunately, as critical a role as the Investment Advisor plays in managing the liquid assets of the nation, little has been done to prepare them for their awesome responsibility. There are no regulatory and/or industry requirements for advanced education and training. Also, the lack of information from regulators on what constitutes an Advisor's investment fiduciary standard of care is unfortunate.

Suggested Procedure

As investment professionals, Advisors have obligations to:

- Be competent

- Place clients' best interests above their own

- Be worthy of the trust placed in them by the investors they serve

It is therefore necessary for Advisors to stay current with, and diligently conform to, best investment practices and legal and regulatory requirements of the profession. Ongoing professional education is a practical necessity and ethical obligation. Advisors should regularly benchmark their activities to the practices addressed in this handbook and commit to ongoing professional development.

CRITERIA

1.1.1 The fiduciary Practices and Procedures defined in this handbook are applied.

PRACTICE A-1.1

THE ADVISOR DEMONSTRATES AN AWARENESS OF FIDUCIARY DUTIES AND RESPONSIBILITIES.

Substantiation

Employee Retirement Income Security Act of 1974 [ERISA]

§404(a)(1)(B)

Case Law
Marshall v. Glass/Metal Association and Glaziers and Glassworkers Pension Plan,
507 F. Supp. 378 2 E.B.C. 1006 (D.Hawaii 1980); *Katsaros v. Cody,* 744 F.2d 270,
5 E.B.C. 1777 (2d Cir. 1984), *cert. denied, Cody v. Donovan,* 469 U.S. 1072, 105 S.
Ct. 565, 83 L.Ed. 2d 506 (1984); *Marshall v. Snyder,* 1 E.B.C. 1878 (E.D.N.Y. 1979);
Donovan v. Mazzola, 716 F.2d 1226, 4 E.B.C. 1865 (9th Cir. 1983), *cert. denied,*
464 U.S. 1040, 104 S. Ct. 704, L.Ed.2d 169 (1984); *Fink v. National Savings and
Trust Company,* 772 F. 2d 951, 6 E.B.C. 2269 (D.C. Cir. 1985)

Other
Joint Committee on Taxation, *Overview of the Enforcement and Administration
of the Employee Retirement and Income Security Act of 1974* (JCX-16-90, June 6,
1990)

Uniform Prudent Investor Act [UPIA]

§1(a); §2(a); §2(d)

Uniform Prudent Management of Institutional Funds Act [UPMIFA]

§3(b); §3(c)

Management of Public Employee Retirement Systems Act [MPERS]

§7

Case Law
National Labor Relations Board v. Amax Coal Co., 453 U.S. 322, 101 S. Ct. 2789,
69 L.Ed. 2d 672 (1981)

INVESTMENTS ARE MANAGED IN ACCORDANCE WITH APPLICABLE LAWS, TRUST DOCUMENTS, AND WRITTEN INVESTMENT POLICY STATEMENTS (IPS).

The starting point for the Investment Advisor is to collect, analyze, and review relevant documents pertaining to the establishment and management of each client's investments. As with the management of any financial decision, the Investment Advisor has to assist the client in establishing definitive goals and objectives. These goals and objectives should be consistent with, but not limited to the following factors:

a. Cash flow

b. Current and future assets

c. Investment experience, expertise, and aptitude

d. Limits and constraints imposed by trust documents (if applicable)

e. Risk tolerance

In addition, if a client is serving as a fiduciary (for a trust, foundation, endowment, or pension plan), then the Investment Advisor must be intimately familiar with all regulations and statutes that define the conduct of the fiduciary client.

Proof that such a framework has been established presumes written documentation exists in some form.

CRITERIA

1.2.1 Investments are managed in accordance with all applicable laws.

1.2.2 Investments held in trust are managed in accordance with client trust documents.

1.2.3 Investments are managed in accordance with each client's written IPS.

1.2.4 Documents pertaining to the investment management process are filed in a centralized location.

Practical Application

The following documents should be collected, reviewed, analyzed, and kept on file for each client:

1. Applicable trust documents (including amendments) [Check to determine whether: (a) trust documents identify trustees and named fiduciaries; (b) trust documents allow for the fiduciaries to prudently delegate investment decisions to others (a provision sometimes found in pre-UPIA trust documents); and (c) documents, statutes, and/or client instructions restrict or prohibit certain asset classes.]

2. A copy of the client's Investment Policy Statement (IPS)

3. In the case of fiduciary clients, written records from investment committee meetings that are pertinent to the advisor's responsibilities

4. Relevant custodial and brokerage agreements

5. Relevant service agreements with other investment service providers (see Practice A-1.3)

6. Information on retained Investment Managers; specifically the ADV for each separate account manager and prospectus for each mutual fund

7. Investment performance reports from Investment Managers, custodians, and/or the previous Investment Advisor

INVESTMENTS ARE MANAGED IN ACCORDANCE WITH APPLICABLE LAWS, TRUST DOCUMENTS, AND WRITTEN INVESTMENT POLICY STATEMENTS (IPS).

Substantiation

Employee Retirement Income Security Act of 1974 [ERISA]

§3(38)(C); §104(b)(4); §402(a)(1); §402(b)(1); §402(b)(2); §403(a); §404(a)(1)(D); §404(b)(2)

Regulations
29 C.F.R. §2509.75-5 FR-4; 29 C.F.R. Interpretive Bulletin 75-5; 29 C.F.R. §2509.94-2(2); 29 C.F.R. Interpretive Bulletin 94-2 (July 29, 1994)

Case Law
Morse v. New York State Teamsters Conference Pension and Retirement Fund, 580 F. Supp. 180 (W.D.N.Y. 1983), aff'd, 761 F.2d 115 (2d Cir. 1985); *Winpisinger v. Aurora Corp. of Illinois*, 456 F. Supp. 559 (N.D. Ohio 1978); Liss v. Smith, 991 F. Supp. 278, 1998 (S.D.N.Y. 1998); *Dardaganis v. Grace Capital, Inc.*, 664 F. Supp. 105 (S.D.N.Y. 1987), aff'd, 889 F.2d 1237 (2d Cir. 1989).

Other
Interpretive Bulletin 75-5, 29 C.F.R. §2509.75-5; Interpretive Bulletin 94-2, 29 C.F.R. §2509.94-2

Uniform Prudent Investor Act [UPIA]

§2(a)–(d); §4

Uniform Prudent Management of Institutional Funds Act [UPMIFA]

§3(b); §3(e)

Management of Public Employee Retirement Systems Act [MPERS]

§4(a)–(d); §7(6); §8(b)

THE ROLES AND RESPONSIBILITIES OF ALL INVOLVED PARTIES (FIDUCIARIES AND NON-FIDUCIARIES) ARE DEFINED, DOCUMENTED, AND ACKNOWLEDGED.

There are numerous parties involved in the investment process, and all of them should have their specific duties and requirements documented, particularly in the client's IPS [See also Practice A-2.6]. This ensures continuity of the investment strategy when there is a change in any of the parties, prevents misunderstandings between parties, and prevents omission of critical fiduciary functions.

The IPS should include sections on:

- The responsibilities of the client and, in the case of the fiduciary client, the role of the investment committee, if any.

- The role of the Investment Advisor.

- The role of the custodian [See also Practice A-3.4].

- The role of the separate account manager(s), if any. [Not necessary for mutual funds, since the investment strategy of the fund already is specified in the fund's prospectus.] The instructions for each money manager should include: (a) securities guidelines, (b) responsibility to seek best price and execution on trading the securities, (c) responsibility to account for soft dollars, and (d) responsibility to vote all proxies [See also Practice A-4.3].

Substantiation

Employee Retirement Income Security Act of 1974 [ERISA]

§3(38)(c); §402(a)(1); §402(b)(2) and (3); §403(a)(2); §404(a)(1)(B); §405(c)(1)

Case Law
Marshall v. Glass/Metal Association and Glaziers and Glassworkers Pension Plan, 507 F. Supp. 378 2 E.B.C. 1006 (D.Hawaii 1980); *Katsaros v. Cody,* 744 F.2d 270, 5 E.B.C. 1777 (2d Cir. 1984), *cert. denied, Cody v. Donovan,* 469 U.S. 1072, 105 S. Ct. 565, 83 L.Ed. 2d 506 (1984); *Marshall v. Snyder,* 1 E.B.C. 1878 (E.D.N.Y. 1979); *Donovan v. Mazzola,* 716 F.2d 1226, 4 E.B.C. 1865 (9th Cir. 1983), *cert. denied,* 464 U.S. 1040, 104 S. Ct. 704, L.Ed.2d 169 (1984); *Fink v. National Savings and Trust Company,* 772 F. 2d 951, 6 E.B.C. 2269 (D.C. Cir. 1985); *Ellis v. Rycenga Homes,* 484 F.Supp.2d 694 (W.D. Mich. 2007)

Other
Joint Committee on Taxation, *Overview of the Enforcement and Administration of the Employee Retirement and Income Security Act of 1974* (JCX-16-90, June 6, 1990)

Uniform Prudent Investor Act [UPIA]

§1(a); §2(a); §2(d); §9(a)(1) and (2)

Other
Restatement of Trusts 3d: Prudent Investor Rule §171 (1992)

Uniform Prudent Management of Institutional Funds Act [UPMIFA]

§3(b); §3(c)

Management of Public Employee Retirement Systems Act [MPERS]

§6(a) and (b); §7; §8(b)

Case Law
National Labor Relations Board v. Amax Coal Co., 453 U.S. 322, 101 S. Ct. 2789, 69 L.Ed. 2d 672 (1981)

CRITERIA

1.3.1 The roles and responsibilities of all parties are documented in the IPS.

1.3.2 All parties demonstrate an awareness of their duties and responsibilities.

1.3.3 All parties have acknowledged their status in writing.

1.3.4 Investment committees have and follow a defined set of by-laws.

PRACTICE A-1.4

THE INVESTMENT ADVISOR IS NOT INVOLVED IN SELF-DEALING AND HAS POLICIES AND PROCEDURES TO ADDRESS SELF-DEALING OF CO-FIDUCIARIES.

CRITERIA

1.4.1 Policies and procedures for overseeing and managing potential conflicts of interests are defined.

1.4.2 All employees annually acknowledge the ethics policies of the Investment Advisor's organization and agree to disclose any potential conflicts of interest.

The fundamental duty of the Investment Advisor is to manage delegated investment decisions for the exclusive benefit of another party (for example the retirement plan participant or the trust beneficiary). In addition, the Advisor has a responsibility to employ an objective independent due diligence process at all times. If a participant or beneficiary is harmed by a decision not conducted at arms length, then a breach is likely to have occurred.

If an Advisor even suspects he or she may have a conflict of interest—they probably do. The best advice is to end the relationship, or avoid it in the first place.

The Investment Advisor should always be asking: Who benefits *most* from an investment decision? If the answer is any party other than the individual investor, plan participant or the beneficiary, then the Advisor is likely to be committing a fiduciary breach.

The Investment Advisor should have defined policies and procedures to manage potential conflicts of interests. Special concerns are raised and additional scrutiny may be required when:

- An Investment Manager or Investment Advisor is associated with a custodian, broker-dealer, and/or shareholder services firm.

- An Investment Manager is acting as a subadvisor to a separately managed account (wrap fee account) and is required to direct trades to a particular broker-dealer.

- An Investment Manager accepts an unusually large number of directed brokerage and commission recapture mandates.

- An Investment Advisor hires an Investment Manager for a reason other than merit.

THE INVESTMENT ADVISOR IS NOT INVOLVED IN SELF-DEALING AND HAS POLICIES AND PROCEDURES TO ADDRESS SELF-DEALING OF CO-FIDUCIARIES.

Suggested Procedure

The Investment Advisor also should be alert to any potential breaches being committed by a fiduciary client. In the event an apparent breach is discovered, the Advisor must notify the client and should consult legal counsel. Examples of possible client fiduciary breaches:

- Using retirement plan assets to buy real estate for corporate use

- Using the assets of a public retirement plan to invest in local high-risk business ventures

- Using the assets of a private trust to provide unsecured loans to related parties and/or entities of the trustee

- Using a company retirement plan as collateral for a line of credit

- Buying artwork and/or other collectibles with retirement plan assets, and putting the collectibles on display

- Trading an account solely to generate additional commissions, also referred to as "churning."

Substantiation

Internal Revenue Code of 1986, as amended [IRC]

§4975

Employee Retirement Income Security Act of 1974 [ERISA]

§3(14)(A) and (B); §404(a)(1)(A); §406(a) and (b)

Case Law
Whitfield v. Tomasso, 682 F. Supp. 1287, 9 E.B.C. 2438 (E.D.N.Y 1988)

Other
DOL Advisory Council on Employee Welfare and Benefit Plans Report of the Working Group on Soft Dollars and Commission Recapture November 13, 1997

Uniform Prudent Investor Act [UPIA]

§2; §5

Uniform Prudent Management of Institutional Funds Act [UPMIFA]

Prefacatory Note

Management of Public Employee Retirement Systems Act [MPERS]

§7(1) and (2); §17(c)(12) and (13)

Practice A-1.5

CRITERIA

1.5.1 Agreements and contracts are periodically reviewed to ensure consistency with the needs of the client.

1.5.2 Agreements and contracts are periodically reviewed by legal counsel.

1.5.3 Consideration is given to putting vendor contracts back out for bid every three years.

Investment Advisors who lack the requisite knowledge required to prudently manage certain investment decisions should seek assistance from outside professionals, such as delegating the construction of stock and bond portfolios to Investment Managers.

When hiring such professionals, any agreement of substance should be reduced to writing in order to define the scope of the parties' duties and responsibilities. This will ensure that the portfolio is managed in accordance with the written documents that govern the investment strategy, and to confirm that the parties have a clear, mutual understanding of their roles and responsibilities.

Suggested Procedure

A good practice is to review contracts and service agreements at least once every three years. The investment industry is constantly evolving, and Investment Advisors may discover:

- There is an opportunity to take advantage of price breaks because the client's portfolio has grown in size.

- The vendor's fees have been reduced because of competitive pressures.

- The scope of services required by the client has changed.

- The vendor's product offering has expanded—the client can benefit from more services without an increase in fees.

- A better vendor has since come to market.

Substantiation

Employee Retirement Income Security Act of 1974 [ERISA]

§3(14)(B) and (38)(C); §3(38)(C); §402(c)(2); §403(a)(2); §404(a)(1); §408(b)(2)

Case Law
Liss v. Smith, 991 F. Supp. 278 (S.D.N.Y. 1998); *Whitfield v. Tomasso,* 682 F. Supp. 1287, 9 E.B.C. 2438 (E.D.N.Y. 1988)

Other
Interpretive Bulletin 94-2, 29 C.F.R. §2509.94-2

Uniform Prudent Investor Act [UPIA]

§2(a); §5; §7; §9(a)(2)

Uniform Prudent Management of Institutional Funds Act [UPMIFA]

§3(b); §3(c); §5(a)

Management of Public Employee Retirement Systems Act [MPERS]

§5(a)(2); §6(b)(2); §7

ASSETS ARE WITHIN THE JURISDICTION OF APPROPRIATE COURTS, AND ARE PROTECTED FROM THEFT AND EMBEZZLEMENT.

The Investment Advisor has the responsibility to safeguard entrusted assets, which also includes keeping the assets within the purview of the relevant judicial system. This gives the courts the ability to seize the assets when they, and/or a regulator, determine the best interests of the client are not being served.

The exception to this Practice is when Investment Advisors are managing the personal assets of an individual client or private trust. They are not precluded from considering the establishment of foreign accounts. However, the Investment Advisor should have a reasonable basis to believe that the assets are within the purview of a viable judicial system. The presumption is that laws will continue to impose appropriate reporting and tracking requirements of foreign bank accounts and trusts.

If the client is an ERISA-qualified retirement plan, Investment Advisors should ensure that a surety bond is in place to reimburse the plan in case dishonest acts result in losses.

Substantiation

Employee Retirement Income Security Act of 1974 [ERISA]

§ 404(b); § 412(a)

Regulations
29 C.F.R. §2550.404b-1

Case Law
Varity Corporation v. Howe, 516 U.S. 489, 116 S. Ct. 1065, 134 L.Ed.2d 130 (1996)

Other
H.R. Report No. 93-1280 (93rd Congress, 2d Session, August 12, 1974)

Uniform Prudent Investor Act [UPIA]

§2(a); §5; §9(d)

Uniform Prudent Management of Institutional Funds Act [UPMIFA]

§3(b); §5(d)

Management of Public Employee Retirement Systems Act [MPERS]

§2(21); §6(e); §7; §11(c) and Comments

CRITERIA

1.6.1 The Investment Advisor has a reasonable basis to believe the assets are within the purview of the relevant judicial system.

1.6.2 ERISA fiduciaries have the required surety bond.

STEP 2: FORMALIZE

PRACTICE A-2.1

AN INVESTMENT TIME HORIZON HAS BEEN IDENTIFIED FOR EACH CLIENT.

CRITERIA

2.1.1 Sources, timing, distribution, and uses of each client's cash flows are documented.

2.1.2 In the case of a defined benefit retirement plan client, the appropriate asset/liability study has been factored into the time horizon.

2.1.3 In the case of a foundation or endowment, the receipt and disbursement of gifts and grants has been factored into the time horizon.

2.1.4 In the case of a retail investor, the appropriate needs-based analysis has been factored into the time horizon.

2.1.5 Sufficient liquid assets for contingency plans are maintained.

Time horizon can be defined as that point-in-time when more money is flowing out of the portfolio than is coming in from contributions and/or from portfolio growth. It is a fundamental duty of the Investment Advisor to ensure there are sufficient liquid assets to pay each client's bills and liabilities when they come due, and to provide a specified level of support when it has been identified.

After determination of the time horizon, the Investment Advisor then can determine which asset classes can be appropriately considered, what the allocation should be between the selected asset classes, and whether there should be an allocation made among sub-asset classes. A short time horizon typically is implemented with fixed income and cash, while a long investment time horizon can be prudently implemented across most asset classes.

AN INVESTMENT TIME HORIZON HAS BEEN IDENTIFIED FOR EACH CLIENT.

Suggested Procedure

One of the most important decisions the Investment Advisor has to make is the time horizon of the investment strategy. Based on the time horizon, the Investment Advisor then can determine: (1) The asset classes to be considered; (2) The mix among the asset classes; (3) The sub-asset classes to be considered; and, finally, (4) The money managers or mutual funds to select.

It is important that the Investment Advisor prepare a schedule of each client's anticipated cash flows so that an appropriate investment time horizon can be identified.

A cash flow schedule provides the Investment Advisor with information to more effectively rebalance a client's asset allocation strategy. For example, if a particular asset class is outside the range of the IPS's strategic limit, the Investment Advisor could use the cash flow information to effectively rebalance the client's portfolio.

The Hierarchy of Decisions

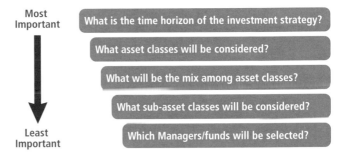

Most Important

Least Important

- What is the time horizon of the investment strategy?
- What asset classes will be considered?
- What will be the mix among asset classes?
- What sub-asset classes will be considered?
- Which Managers/funds will be selected?

Substantiation

Employee Retirement Income Security Act of 1974 [ERISA]

§404(a)(1)(B)

Regulations
29 C.F.R. §2550.404a-1(b)(1)(A); 29 C.F.R. §2550.404a-1(b)(2)(A)

Case Law
Metzler v. Graham, 112 F.3d 207, 20 E.B.C. 2857 (5th Cir. 1997)

Other
Interpretive Bulletin 96-1, 29 C.F.R. §2509.96-1; H.R. Report No. 1280, 93d Congress, 2d Session (1974)

Uniform Prudent Investor Act [UPIA]

§2(a); §2(b)

Uniform Prudent Management of Institutional Funds Act [UPMIFA]

§3

Management of Public Employee Retirement Systems Act [MPERS]

§8; §10(b)

PRACTICE A-2.2

CRITERIA

2.2.1 The level of risk the client's portfolio is exposed to is understood, and the quantitative and qualitative factors that were considered are documented.

2.2.2 A "worst-case" scenario has been considered, and it has been determined that the portfolio has sufficient liquidity to meet short-term (less than five years) obligations.

The term "risk" has different connotations, depending on an Investment Advisor's and/or a client's frame of reference, circumstances, and objectives. Typically, the investment industry defines risk in terms of statistical measures such as standard deviation. However, these statistical measures may fail to adequately communicate the potential negative consequences an investment strategy can have on the client's ability to meet investment objectives.

An investment strategy can fail by being too conservative or too aggressive. An Investment Advisor could adopt a "safe" investment strategy by keeping a portfolio in cash, but then see the portfolio's purchasing power whither under inflation. Or a long-term growth strategy could be implemented that overexposes a portfolio to equities, when a more conservative fixed-income strategy would be sufficient to cover the identified goals and objectives.

Suggested Procedure

One suggested approach is to stress test a client's proposed investment strategy by analyzing possible outcomes (worst case, most likely, and best case) over one-, three-, and five-year (or longer) periods. The Investment Advisor should then consider the possible consequences of each outcome:

1. Will the investment results enable the client to cover short- and long-term liabilities and/or objectives?

2. Can the client stomach the worst-case scenario? If not, the client will likely abandon a sound, long-term strategy during a market downturn; altering the investment strategy at precisely the wrong time and for the wrong reasons.

A RISK LEVEL HAS BEEN IDENTIFIED FOR EACH CLIENT.

Modeled Worst Case Scenario

A modeled worst case scenario can be represented visually in a number of different ways, one of which is shown here:

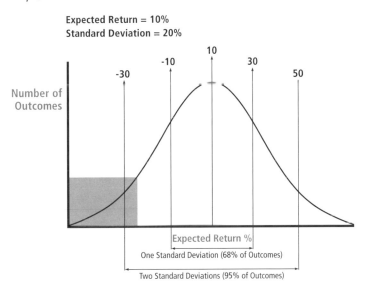

Substantiation

Employee Retirement Income Security Act of 1974 [ERISA]

§404(a)(1)(B)

Regulations
29 C.F.R. §2550.404a-1(b)(1)(A); 29 C.F.R. §2550.404a-1(b)(2)(B)(i-iii)

Case Law
Laborers National Pension Fund v. Northern Trust Quantitative Advisors, Inc.,
173 F.3d 313, 23 E.B.C. 1001 (5th Cir.), *reh'g and reh'g en banc denied,* 184 F.3d
820 (5th Cir.), *cert. denied,* 528 U.S. 967, 120 S.Ct. 406, 145 L.Ed.2d 316 (1999);
Chase v. Pevear, 383 Mass. 350, 419 N.E.2d 1358 (1981)

Uniform Prudent Investor Act [UPIA]

§2(b) and (c); §2 Comments

Uniform Prudent Management of Institutional Funds Act [UPMIFA]

§3(e)

Management of Public Employee Retirement Systems Act [MPERS]

§8(b); §8 Comments

AN EXPECTED, MODELED RETURN TO MEET INVESTMENT OBJECTIVES HAS BEEN IDENTIFIED.

The Investment Advisor should determine whether trust documents, spending policies, and/or actuarial reports (for defined benefit retirement plans) establish a minimum investment return expectation or requirement. In all cases, the Investment Advisor should determine the "modeled," or expected, return a given investment strategy is likely to produce, and whether it meets the client's stated investment goals and objectives.

In this context, the term "model" means to replicate: to determine the probable returns of an investment strategy given current and historical information. There is no fiduciary requirement, or expectation, that the Investment Advisor be capable of forecasting future returns. Rather, they are required to demonstrate the prudent process that was followed in developing the assumptions used to model the probable outcomes of a range of investment strategies.

Suggested Procedure

An optimizer requires three inputs:

> Expected Return—the *modeled* return assumption that will be used for each asset class.
>
> Standard Deviation—the *probable* level of variability each asset class will exhibit.
>
> Correlation Coefficient—the *estimate* of the degree to which each asset class will perform relative to another. (Historically, equities and fixed-income asset returns have not been similar over the same periods of time; therefore, they would have a relatively low correlation to one another.)

Note that all three optimizer variables are nothing more than estimates, models, or probable outcomes. The asset allocation strategy must be built upon carefully developed expectations for the capital markets and the way in which individual asset classes are expected to perform in relation to, and in combination with, each other. Further constraints on asset classes may be required to comply with the client's investment policy statement and to generate meaningful allocations.

The development of sound optimizer inputs involves as much art and intuition as science, and is well beyond the intended scope of this handbook. However, the Investment Advisor is advised to be familiar with the source and methodology used to develop any asset allocation strategy. Due to the great disparity between different models, careful research into the investment expertise of the source is required.

CRITERIA

2.3.1 The "expected" or "modeled" return for each client is consistent with the client's investment goals and objectives.

2.3.2 The "expected" or "modeled" return assumptions for each asset class are based on risk-premium assumptions, as opposed to recent short-term performance.

2.3.3 For defined benefit plans, the expected return values used for actuarial calculations are reasonable.

AN EXPECTED, MODELED RETURN TO MEET INVESTMENT OBJECTIVES HAS BEEN IDENTIFIED.

The outputs of the computerized optimization models are only as good as the inputs. The old adage "garbage in—garbage out" has never been more applicable.

The modeling of a probable return for a given asset allocation strategy is very difficult to develop. Simple extrapolations of recent historical data may be poor estimates of future performance, they also may cause the Investment Advisor to overweight an asset class that has had recent superior performance and underweight the laggards, setting the stage for the Investment Advisor to make the classic investment mistake— buying high and selling low.

Many investment professionals use "risk-premium" adjusted inputs in an optimizer, as opposed to historical data. Developing the risk premium is quite involved but, simply stated, the process starts by calculating the premium each asset class has earned over the risk-free-rate-of-return. The premium is then adjusted, or tweaked, based on possible economic scenarios that may impact the asset class over the next five years. The adjusted premium is then added to the anticipated risk-free rate-of-return over the next five years (the anticipated rate of inflation also could be used as a proxy) to come up with the final modeled return. The Investment Advisor should consider carefully whether the risk premiums used are reasonable, as the asset allocation output can be quite sensitive to the input values.

Substantiation

Employee Retirement Income Security Act of 1974 [ERISA]

§404(a)(1)(A) and (B)

Regulations
29 C.F.R. §2550.404a-1(b)(1)(A); 29 C.F.R. §2550.404a-1(b)(2)(A)

Case Law
Federal Power Commission v. Hope Natural Gas Company, 320 U.S. 591, 64 S.Ct. 281, 88 L.Ed. 333 (1944); *Communications Satellite Corporation v. Federal Communications Commission,* 611 F.2d 883 (D.C. Cir. 1977); *Tennessee Gas Pipeline Company v. Federal Energy Regulatory Commission,* 926 F.2d 1206 (D.C. Cir. 1991)

Uniform Prudent Investor Act [UPIA]

§2(b); §2(c)(1-8)

Uniform Prudent Management of Institutional Funds Act [UPMIFA]

§3(e)

Management of Public Employee Retirement Systems Act [MPERS]

§8(a)(1)(A-F); §8(b)

PRACTICE A-2.4

SELECTED ASSET CLASSES ARE CONSISTENT WITH THE RISK, RETURN, AND TIME HORIZON.

The Investment Advisor's role is to choose the appropriate combination of asset classes that optimizes each client's identified risk and return objectives, consistent with the client's time horizon. The Investment Advisor's choice of asset classes and subsequent allocation typically will have more impact on the long-term performance of the client's investment strategy than the selection of money managers.

CRITERIA

2.4.1 Assets are appropriately diversified to conform to each client's specified time horizon and risk/return profile.

2.4.2 For participant directed plans, selected asset classes provide each participant the ability to diversify their portfolio appropriately given their time horizon and risk/return profile.

2.4.3 The methodology and tools used to establish appropriate portfolio diversification for each client are effective and consistently applied.

Suggested Procedure

Computer optimization models can mathematically assist the Investment Advisor in determining alternative optimal asset mixes. Yet these technological tools and comprehensive databases have not reduced the asset allocation decision to a computerized, mathematical solution. The acronym "TREAT" helps to define the key inputs to a client's asset allocation strategy.

T Time horizon of the client (Practice 2.1)

R Risk level of the client (Practice 2.2)

E Expected return necessary to meet client's goals and objectives (Practice 2.3)

A Asset class preferences of the client

T Tax status of the client

Substantiation

Employee Retirement Income Security Act of 1974 [ERISA]

§404(a)(1)(B)

Regulations
29 C.F.R. §2550.404a-1; 29 C.F.R. §2550.404a-1(b)(1)(A); 29 C.F.R. §2550.404a-1(b)(2)(B)(i-iii)

Case Law
GIW Industries, Inc. v. Trevor, Stewart, Burton & Jacobsen, Inc., 895 F.2d 729 (11th Cir. 1990); Leigh v. Engle, 858 F.2d 361 (7th Cir. 1988)

Other
Interpretive Bulletin 96-1, 29 C.F.R. §2509.96-1

Uniform Prudent Investor Act [UPIA]

§2(b)

Uniform Prudent Management of Institutional Funds Act [UPMIFA]

§3

Management of Public Employee Retirement Systems Act [MPERS]

§8(b)

SELECTED ASSET CLASSES ARE CONSISTENT WITH IMPLEMENTATION AND MONITORING CONSTRAINTS.

The number of asset classes should be consistent with the Investment Advisor's (in some cases, client's) implementation and monitoring constraints. No formula can determine the best number of asset classes—the appropriate number is determined by facts and circumstances. How many asset classes should be considered? Or in the case of participant-directed retirement plans, how many investment options should be offered? The answer is dependent on certain variables:

- Size of the client's portfolio

- Investment expertise of the client and/or Investment Advisor

- Ability of the Investment Advisor to properly monitor the strategies and/or investment options

- Sensitivity to investment expenses—more asset classes and/or options may mean higher portfolio expenses. The additional costs of added diversification should be evaluated in light of the price the client pays for being less diversified

- Suitability of the asset class to the client

Suggested Procedure

Ordinarily, the most appropriate asset classes to be used as a starting point are the broad market classes representing the full range of investment opportunities. Simply stated: stocks, bonds, and cash. From this starting point, additional asset classes, sub asset classes and/or peer groups should be added to   provide meaningful risk and return benefits to the overall investment strategy. This is based on the premise that the client's time horizon is greater than five years.

The Investment Advisor should keep in mind that the allocation also must be implemented and monitored. It makes no sense to make an allocation to an asset class that can not be effectively and efficiently implemented and/or monitored on an ongoing basis.

CRITERIA

2.5.1 The Advisor has the time, inclination, and knowledge to effectively implement and monitor all selected asset classes for each client.

2.5.2 The process and tools used to implement and monitor investments in the selected asset classes are effective.

2.5.3 The ability to access suitable investment products within all selected asset classes has been considered.

SELECTED ASSET CLASSES ARE CONSISTENT WITH IMPLEMENTATION AND MONITORING CONSTRAINTS.

Substantiation

Employee Retirement Income Security Act of 1974 [ERISA]

§404(a)(1)(C)

Other

H.R. Report No. 1280, 93rd Congress, 2d Sess.304, reprinted in 1974 U.S. Code Cong. & Admin. News 5038 (1974)

Uniform Prudent Investor Act [UPIA]

§2(b)

Other

Restatement of Trusts 3d: Prudent Investor Rule §227, comment

Uniform Prudent Management of Institutional Funds Act [UPMIFA]

§3(e)

Management of Public Employee Retirement Systems Act [MPERS]

§8(a)(1); §8(a)(4); §10(2)

There is an IPS which contains the detail to define, implement, and monitor the client's investment strategy.

The preparation and maintenance of each client's IPS is one of the most critical functions performed by the Investment Advisor. The IPS should be viewed as the business plan and the essential management tool for directing and communicating the activities of each client's portfolio. It should be a formal, long-range, strategic plan that allows the Investment Advisor to coordinate the management of each client's investment program in a logical and consistent framework. All material investment facts, assumptions, and opinions should be included.

The Investment Advisor is required to manage investment decisions with a reasonable level of detail. By reducing the details to writing and preparing a written IPS, the Investment Advisor can: (1) avoid unnecessary differences of opinion and the resulting conflicts with clients, (2) minimize the possibility of missteps due to a lack of clear guidelines, (3) establish a reasoned basis for measuring success, both in terms of meeting the client's objectives and the Investment Advisor's efforts, and (4) establish and communicate reasonable and clear expectations with clients.

There are a number of benefits from having a well-written IPS:

- It supports the "paper trail" in the event of an audit, litigation, and or a dispute. One of the first documents a litigator or auditor is likely to review is the IPS, because it should provide an outline of the client's overall investment strategy.

- It helps to insulate the Investment Advisor and the client from "market noise." During periods of over- and under-confidence in the capital markets, the IPS helps to keep the client focused on the long-term goals and objectives.

- It helps to provide implementation guidance during estate planning, particularly when one spouse is still actively managing all or a significant portion of the investable assets. Often, it's the "investing spouse" who is the first to become incapacitated, leaving the surviving spouse and/or executor with the near impossible task of continuing the former investment strategy. An IPS thoughtfully prepared in advance and integrated within the overall estate plan would help to ensure the smooth transition of the investment strategy.

The IPS should have sufficient detail that a competent third party could implement the investment strategy, be flexible enough that it can be implemented in a complex and dynamic financial environment, and yet not be so detailed as to require constant revisions and updates. Addendums could be used to identify client information that will change on a more frequent basis, such as the capital markets assumptions used to develop the client's asset allocation and the names of board members, accountants, attorneys, actuaries, and money managers/mutual funds.

One of the challenges of writing an IPS is to create investment guidelines specific enough to clearly establish the parameters of the desired investment process, yet provide enough latitude so as not to create an oversight burden. This is particularly true when establishing the client's asset allocation and rebalancing limits.

CRITERIA

2.6.1 Each client's IPS defines the duties and responsibilities of all parties involved.

2.6.2 Each client's IPS defines diversification and rebalancing guidelines consistent with specified risk, return, time horizon, and cash flow parameters.

2.6.3 Each client's IPS defines the due diligence criteria for selecting investment options.

2.6.4 Each client's IPS defines the monitoring criteria for investment options and service vendors.

2.6.5 Each client's IPS defines procedures for controlling and accounting for investment expenses.

THERE IS AN IPS WHICH CONTAINS THE DETAIL TO DEFINE, IMPLEMENT, AND MONITOR THE CLIENT'S INVESTMENT STRATEGY.

Rebalancing is required to maintain proper diversification, where the goal is to ensure that the client's portfolio does not stray far from its targeted levels of risk and return. An optimal portfolio can only be maintained by periodically rebalancing the portfolio to maintain the appropriate diversification.

By establishing specific asset allocation parameters and money manager (or mutual fund) selection criteria, it is much easier to determine whether a prospective manager fits into the approved investment program. The Investment Advisor should investigate the qualities, characteristics, and merits of each money manager, and identify the role each plays in the implementation of the client's investment strategy. However, such an investigation and the related analysis cannot be conducted in a vacuum—it must be within the context of the needs of the investment strategy. Once the needs have been defined, and the general strategies developed, specific money managers should be chosen within the context of this strategy.

The Investment Advisor's duty to monitor the performance of Investment Managers and other service providers is inherent in the obligations of fiduciaries to act prudently in carrying out their duties. Specific performance criteria and objectives should be identified for each money manager and/or mutual fund.

Investment Advisors also must establish procedures for controlling and accounting for investment expenses. An Investment Advisor has a duty to ensure that their client incurs only reasonable and necessary expenses.

There is an IPS which contains the detail to define, implement, and monitor the client's investment strategy.

Substantiation

Employee Retirement Income Security Act of 1974 [ERISA]

§402(c)(3); §404(a); §406(a)(1)(C); §408(b)(2)

Regulations
29 C.F.R. §2550.404a-1(b)(1)(A); §2550.404a-1(b)(2)(i); 29 C.F.R. §2550.404a-1(b)(2)

Case Law
In re Unisys Savings Plan Litigation, 74 F.3d 420, 19 E.B.C. 2393 (3rd Cir.), *cert. denied,* 510 U.S. 810, 117 S.Ct. 56, 136 L.Ed.2d 19 (1996); *Morrissey v. Curran,* 567 F.2d 546, 1 E.B.C. 1659 (2nd Cir. 1977); *Harley v. Minnesota Mining and Manufacturing Company,* 42 F. Supp.2d 898 (D.Minn. 1999), aff'd, 284 F.3d 901 (8th Cir. 2002); *Whitfield v. Cohen,* 682 F. Supp. 188, 9 E.B.C. 1739 (S.D.N.Y. 1988); *Liss v. Smith,* 991 F.Supp. 278 (S.D.N.Y. 1988); *Leigh v. Engle,* 858 F.2d 361, 10 E.B.C. 1041 (7th Cir. 1988), *cert. denied,* 489 U.S. 1078, 109 S.Ct. 1528, 103 L.Ed.2d 833 (1989)

Other
Interpretive Bulletin 94-2, 29 C.F.R. §2509.94-2; Interpretive Bulletin 75-8, 29 C.F.R. §2509.75-8; Interpretive Bulletin 96-1, 29 C.F.R. §2509.96-1(e); H.R. Report No. 1280, 93rd Cong. 2d Sess. 304, reprinted in 1974 U.S. Code Cong. & Admin. News 5038 (1974)

Uniform Prudent Investor Act [UPIA]

§2(a-b); §2 Comments; §3 and Comments; §4; §7; §9(a)(1), (2) and (3)

Other
Restatement of Trusts 3d: Prudent Investor Rule §227(a); OCC Interpretive Letter No. 722 (March 12, 1996), citing the Restatement of Trusts 3d: Prudent Investor Rule §227, comment m at 58 (1992)

Uniform Prudent Management of Institutional Funds Act [UPMIFA]

§3(c); §3(e); §5(a)

Management of Public Employee Retirement Systems Act [MPERS]

§6(b)(2) and (3); 7(2), (3) and (5); §7(5) and Comments; §8(a); §8 and Comments

Other
Restatement of Trusts 3d: Prudent Investor Rule §227, comment g

PRACTICE A-2.7

CRITERIA

2.7.1 Each client's goals and objectives have been evaluated to determine whether socially responsible investing is appropriate and/or desirable.

2.7.2 If a client has elected to implement a socially responsible investment strategy, the client's IPS is appropriately structured, implemented, and monitored.

There is increasing interest by some clients to incorporate social, ethical, moral, and/or religious criteria into their investment strategy—to align investment decisions with the client's core values. There are two terms that are used interchangeably by the industry: mission-based investing and socially responsible investing (SRI).

Generally speaking, fiduciary standards of care cannot be abrogated to accommodate the pursuit of a SRI strategy. (Of course, the individual investor has no such constraints.) However, in the case of fiduciary clients that fall under the UPIA (personal trusts, foundations, and endowments), failure to consider an SRI strategy could be a breach if:

- The trust documents establishing the private trust, foundation, or endowment state that SRI is preferred.

- A donor directs the use of a SRI strategy as a condition for making a donation.

- A reasonable person would deduce from the foundation's/endowment's mission that SRI would be considered (e.g., it is reasonable to assume that the American Cancer Society would avoid investing in tobacco companies).

> **Sample Language for the IPS**
>
> *The manager is instructed to evaluate all investment options according to objective economic criteria established by the manager and, if there are equally attractive investments, social factors may be considered.*

The IPS defines appropriately structured, socially responsible investment (SRI) strategies (where applicable).

Suggested Procedure

There are a number of different approaches the client can employ to execute mission-based and SRI strategies. Some strategies may not be legally suitable for all clients and certain fiduciary clients should consult legal counsel before adopting an SRI approach. The following is a brief synopsis:

1. The client may wish to direct the Investment Advisor to find money managers or mutual funds that incorporate particular SRI screens. The screens may be either inclusionary or exclusionary. Inclusionary qualitative screens might include companies that emphasize:

   - Product quality/consumer relations
   - Environmental performance
   - Community relations
   - Diversity
   - Employee relations

   Exclusionary screens might include:

   - The "sin" stocks—alcohol, tobacco, firearms
   - Nuclear power
   - Military weapons
   - Life ethics

2. The client may wish to pursue a strategy of shareholder activism—actually purchasing shares of stock in a targeted company so that the client can participate in corporate governance activities.

3. The client may wish to pursue Economically-Targeted Investing (ETI). ETI is the use of portfolio assets to produce collateral benefits such as jobs, housing loans, and venture capital.

4. The client may wish to direct the Investment Advisor to find money managers that are minority and/or women-owned business enterprises.

In the case of ERISA clients, the key to successfully incorporating an SRI strategy is to demonstrate that prospective investment results are not negatively impacted. It has become a generally accepted practice to permit the inclusion of an SRI strategy as a secondary screen to a normal (unrestricted) investment process. If there are equally attractive investment options, then social factors may be considered.

If the client is a participant-directed defined contribution plan, the most prudent way to implement an SRI investment option is to present the SRI investment option alongside a general purpose fund of the same peer group. This way, each participant can choose whether or not to elect SRI.

THE IPS DEFINES APPROPRIATELY STRUCTURED, SOCIALLY RESPONSIBLE INVESTMENT (SRI) STRATEGIES (WHERE APPLICABLE).

Substantiation

Employee Retirement Income Security Act of 1974 [ERISA]

§403(c)(1); §404(a)(1)

Other
ERISA Opinion Letter 98-04A (May 28, 1998); Interpretive Bulletin 94-1, 29 C.F.R. §2509.94-1

Uniform Prudent Investor Act [UPIA]

§2(a); §2(c); §5

Uniform Prudent Management of Institutional Funds Act [UPMIFA]

§3(b); §3(e)

Management of Public Employee Retirement Systems Act [MPERS]

§7(1), (2) and (3); §8(a) (1) and (2); §8(a)(5); §8(b)

United Nations' Principles for Responsible Investment

In 2005, the United Nations Secretary-General convened an international group of institutional investors to reflect on the increasing relevance of ESG issues to investment practices. The outgrowth of the study was the release of the six "Principles for Responsible Investment":

1. We will incorporate ESG issues into investment analysis and decision-making processes.

2. We will be active owners and incorporate ESG issues into our ownership policies and practices.

3. We will seek appropriate disclosure on ESG issues by the entities in which we invest.

4. We will promote acceptance and implementation of the Principles within the investment industry.

5. We will work together to enhance our effectiveness in implementing the Principles.

6. We will each report on our activities and progress towards implementing the Principles.

STEP 3: IMPLEMENT

EACH CLIENT'S INVESTMENT STRATEGY IS IMPLEMENTED IN COMPLIANCE WITH THE REQUIRED LEVEL OF PRUDENCE.

Investment Advisors will be held to an "expert standard of care" and their activities and conduct will be measured accordingly. The primary role of the Investment Advisor is to manage the client's investment process, not to make investment decisions such as individual stock and bonds. It is the role of professional money managers to manage the portfolio. The Investment Advisor can be far more effective and efficient spending his or her time managing the managers.

Therefore, there is a great emphasis on the due diligence process an Investment Advisor should develop in selecting money managers. Whether investment decisions are delegated to professionals (strongly encouraged) or retained by the Investment Advisor, the Advisor should demonstrate that a due diligence process was followed in selecting each investment option.

CRITERIA

3.1.1 A due diligence procedure for selecting investment options exists.

3.1.2 The due diligence process is consistently applied.

Suggested Procedure

As a general rule, a fiduciary should develop due diligence criteria with the following in mind:

1. Develop a process that can be applied to both mutual funds and separate account managers, so that the Advisor can easily migrate from one universe to another.

2. Develop a process that can be applied to any of the readily available databases on mutual funds and/or separate account managers.

3. Develop a simple process that can easily be understood by clients and replicated outside of the office.

4. Develop screens that can serve a dual purpose—apply to searches as well as to monitoring.

When managers or funds are selected without following a due diligence process, there are potential problems:

1. Important search criteria can be omitted.

2. Performance may be compared to inappropriate indexes or peer groups.

3. Information provided by the manager or fund may focus on what the manager or fund wants the Advisor to hear, and not necessarily what the Advisor needs to know.

EACH CLIENT'S INVESTMENT STRATEGY IS IMPLEMENTED IN COMPLIANCE WITH THE REQUIRED LEVEL OF PRUDENCE.

SUGGESTED FIELDS OF DUE DILIGENCE	Threshold Defined by fi360	Threshold Defined by Fiduciary	IPS (Practice 2.6)	Implement (Practice 3.1)	Monitor (Practice 4.1)
			Due diligence is reflected in procedures		
1. Regulatory oversight	Each investment option should be managed by: (a) a bank, (b) an insurance company, (c) a registered investment company (mutual fund), or (d) a registered investment adviser.				
2. Minimum track record	Each investment option should have at least three years of history so that performance statistics can be properly calculated.				
3. Stability of the organization	The same portfolio management team should be in place for at least two years.				
4. Assets in the product	Each investment option should have at least $75 million under management (for mutual funds - can include assets in related share classes).				
5. Holdings consistent with style	At least 80% of the underlying securities should be consistent with the broad asset class.				
6. Correlation to style or peer group	Each investment option should be highly correlated to the asset class being implemented.				
7. Expense ratios/fees	Fees should not be in the bottom quartile (most expensive) of the peer group.				
8. Performance relative to assumed risk	The investment option's risk - adjusted performance (Alpha and/or Sharpe Ratio) should be evaluated against the peer group median manager's risk-adjusted performance.				
9. Performance relative to a peer group	Each investment option's performance should be evaluated against the peer group's median manager return, for 1-, 3-, and 5-year cumulative periods.				
10. Other					
11. Other					

EACH CLIENT'S INVESTMENT STRATEGY IS IMPLEMENTED IN COMPLIANCE WITH THE REQUIRED LEVEL OF PRUDENCE.

Substantiation

Employee Retirement Income Security Act of 1974 [ERISA]

§402(c)(3); §403(a)(1) and (2); §404(a)(1)(B)

Regulations

29 C.F.R. §2550.404a-1(b)(1) and (2)

Case Law
Howard v. Shay, 100 F.3d 1484, 20 E.B.C. 2097 (9th Cir. 1996), *cert. denied,* 520 U.S. 1237, 117 S.Ct. 1838, 137 L.Ed.2d 1042 (1997); *Fink v. National Savings and Trust Co.,* 772 F.2d 951 (D.C. Cir. 1985); *Katsaros v. Cody,* 744 F.2d 270, 5 E.B.C. 1777 (2nd Cir.), *cert. denied,* 469 U.S. 1072, 105 S.Ct. 565, 83 L.Ed.2d 506 (1984); *Donovan v. Mazzola,* 716 F.2d 1226 (9th Cir. 1983), *cert. denied,* 464 U.S. 1040, 104 S.Ct. 704, 79 L.Ed.2d 169 (1984); *United States v. Mason Tenders Dist. Council of Greater New York,* 909 F.Supp. 882, 19 E.B.C. 1467 (S.D.N.Y. 1995); *Trapani v. Consolidated Edison Employees' Mutual Aid Society,* 693 F.Supp. 1509 (S.D.N.Y. 1988)

Uniform Prudent Investor Act [UPIA]

§2(c); §2(f); *§9(a)(1-3)*

Uniform Prudent Management of Institutional Funds Act [UPMIFA]

§3(b); 5(a)

Management of Public Employee Retirement Systems Act [MPERS]

§6(a); §6(b)(1); §6(b)(3); §7(3); §8(a)(1)

PRACTICE A-3.2

WHEN SAFE HARBORS ARE ELECTED, EACH CLIENT'S INVESTMENT STRATEGY IS IMPLEMENTED IN COMPLIANCE WITH THE APPLICABLE PROVISIONS.

There are three important concepts associated with each of the safe harbor procedures summarized in this Practice:

1. They are voluntary—the procedures are not compulsory for the Steward. However, a Steward choosing not to seek an available safe harbor bears the risk and consequences. Similarly, the Advisor who, in the role of consultant to the plan, does not advise a Steward of safe harbor opportunities could face co-liability for the Steward's breaches.

2. They may insulate the Steward (and possibly the Advisor/consultant) from liability associated with certain investment-related decisions and acts. The Steward should think of safe harbor procedures as a form of "insurance."

3. They require the Steward to demonstrate compliance with the applicable defined requirements. Applicable, in this case, meaning those provisions directly affecting the investment decision making process. (The question of "literal" versus "substantial" *compliance* will be answered by the courts.)

There are four distinct safe harbors available to Investment Fiduciaries:

1. The 404(a) Safe Harbor, or general safe harbor provisions related to delegation of investment decisions

2. The 404(c) Safe Harbor
   (applicable only to ERISA Investment Stewards)

3. The Fiduciary Adviser Safe Harbor
   (applicable only to ERISA Investment Stewards)

4. The Qualified Default Investment Alternative (QDIA) Safe Harbor

404(a) Delegation of Investment Decisions Safe Harbor Requirements

When investment decisions are delgated (regardless of being in a participant-directed or committee-directed plan); there are five generally recognized safe harbor requirements.

1. Investment decisions must be delegated to a "prudent expert(s)" (registered investment adviser [including mutual funds], bank, or insurance company).

2. The Investment Steward must demonstrate that the prudent expert(s) was selected by following a due diligence process.

3. The prudent expert(s) must be given discretion over the assets.

4. The prudent expert(s) must acknowledge their co-fiduciary status in writing (mutual funds are exempted from this requirement—the prospectus is deemed to serve as the fund's fiduciary acknowledgment).

WHEN SAFE HARBORS ARE ELECTED, EACH CLIENT'S INVESTMENT STRATEGY IS IMPLEMENTED IN COMPLIANCE WITH THE APPLICABLE PROVISIONS.

5. The Investment Steward must monitor the activities of the prudent expert(s) to ensure that the expert(s) is properly performing the agreed upon tasks using the agreed upon criteria.

[Note: UPIA, UPMIFA, and MPERS also include language that provides a certain degree of protection for fiduciaries who properly delegate investment responsibility.]

404(c) Safe Harbor Requirements

When investment decisions are participant-directed, as in the case of the typical 401(k) plan, there are nine requirements. These safe harbor requirements are more commonly referred to as 404(c) requirements. There are several proposed amendments to these procedures which have been introduced by the 2006 Pension Protection Act (PPA).

The first five requirements are identical to those of the committee-directed safe harbor, a point that should not be lost on plan fiduciaries. Many 401(k) Investment Stewards have mistakenly assumed that they were relieved of many (if not all) of their fiduciary responsibilities when they elected to allow participants to manage their own investment decisions. This simply is not the case.

Requirements 1-5 (see page 46), same as for committee-directed investment decisions

6. Plan participants must be notified in writing that the plan sponsor intends to constitute a 404(c) plan, and seek liability relief through these safe harbor procedures.

7. Participants must be offered at least three investment options with materially different risk/return profiles.

8. Participants must receive information and education on the different investment options.

9. Participants must be provided the opportunity to change their investment strategy/allocation with a frequency that is appropriate in light of market volatility.

Fiduciary Adviser Safe Harbor Requirements

The PPA defines a safe harbor for Investment Stewards who want to provide specific investment advice to 401(k) plan participants, and defines two terms that are related to the safe harbor requirements: "fiduciary adviser" and "eligible investment advice arrangement":

> A "fiduciary adviser" is a person who is providing specific investment advice to plan participants.

> An "eligible investment advice arrangement," is either a computer-driven advice model and/or fee neutral. (The fiduciary adviser's compensation is not impacted by which fund family, fund, share class, and/or asset mix is suggested.)

WHEN SAFE HARBORS ARE ELECTED, EACH CLIENT'S INVESTMENT STRATEGY IS IMPLEMENTED IN COMPLIANCE WITH THE APPLICABLE PROVISIONS.

The new fiduciary adviser safe harbor requirements are:

1. The Investment Steward must prudently select a qualified fiduciary adviser.

2. The fiduciary adviser must acknowledge to the Investment Steward and each participant fiduciary status in writing, disclose all conflicts of interests, and all forms of compensation.

3. The Investment Steward must determine that the fiduciary adviser's "eligible investment advice arrangement," including the associated fees and expenses, is appropriate for the plan's participants.

4. The Investment Steward must prudently monitor the fiduciary adviser, and ensure that both the procedural prudence of the fiduciary adviser, and the "eligible investment advice arrangement," are audited on an annual basis.

Qualified Default Investment Alternative Safe Harbor Requirements

A plan sponsor can avoid liability for participant investment decisions by offering a "qualified default investment alternative," defined as:

1. Age-based life-cycle or targeted retirement date funds or accounts;

2. Risk-based, balanced funds; or

3. An investment management service.

Participants must be provided:

1. Details of the "alternative."

2. "Notification" 30 days in advance of the first investment and each subsequent year, of the opportunity to transfer assets to any other investment alternative available without financial penalty.

Employer stock is permissible if:

1. The stock is held or acquired by a registered investment company or pooled investment vehicle that is independent of the employer.

2. The stock is acquired as a matching contribution from the employer and the stock is held at the direction of the particpant.

WHEN SAFE HARBORS ARE ELECTED, EACH CLIENT'S INVESTMENT STRATEGY IS IMPLEMENTED IN COMPLIANCE WITH THE APPLICABLE PROVISIONS.

Substantiation

Employee Retirement Income Security Act of 1974 [ERISA]

§402(c)(3); §404(a) and (c); §405(d)(1); §404(c)(4); §404(c)(5)

Regulations
29 C.F.R. §2550.404a-1; 29 C.F.R. §2550.404a-1(b)(1) and (2)

Other
Interpretive Bulletin 75-8, 29 C.F.R. §2509.75-8 (FR-17Q); Interpretive Bulletin 94-2, 29 C.F.R. §2509.94-2; DOL Miscellaneous Document, 4/13/98 – Study of 401(k) Plan Fees and Expenses; Fed. Reg., Vol. 44, p. 37255

Case Law
Tittle v. Enron Corp., 284 F.Supp.2d 511, 578 (S.D. Texas 2003)

Uniform Prudent Investor Act [UPIA]

§9(a); §9(c)

Uniform Prudent Management of Institutional Funds Act [UPMIFA]

§5(a); 5(c)

Management of Public Employee Retirement Systems Act [MPERS]

§6(b); §6(d)

INVESTMENT VEHICLES ARE APPROPRIATE FOR THE PORTFOLIO SIZE.

The primary focus of this Practice is the implementation of the investment strategy with appropriate investment vehicles.

It is important for the Investment Advisor to be familiar with the universe of investment options (mutual funds, ETFs, and separate account managers to illustrate the more common investment vehicles), for no one implementation structure is right for all occasions.

There are numerous factors that should be considered in the selection of an investment vehicle, including:

- Ease of liquidity
- Minimum required investment
- The degree to which the investment is diversified
- Ease in meeting asset allocation and rebalancing guidelines
- Ability to perform the appropriate due diligence
- Flexibility in adjusting fees for growing or larger portfolios
- Ability to fund with assets-in-kind
- Built-in (phantom) tax issues
- Tax efficiency – ability to manage the tax consequences of low-basis and/or restricted stock
- Degree of portfolio transparency
- Whether portfolio and performance information is audited
- Degree of regulatory oversight
- Ability to give investment direction to the portfolio manager
- Deductibility of management fees
- Cost

Investment Advisors also should be able to demonstrate that they thoughtfully considered whether to implement passive versus active investment strategies. This duty is related to the Investment Advisor's responsibilities to (1) act as a prudent expert, and (2) control and account for investment expenses.

CRITERIA

3.3.1 Decisions regarding passive and active investment strategies are documented and appropriately implemented.

3.3.2 Decisions regarding the use of separately managed and commingled accounts, such as mutual funds and unit trusts, are documented and appropriately implemented.

3.3.3 Regulated investment options are selected over unregulated options when comparable risk and return characteristics are projected.

3.3.4 Investment options that are covered by readily available data sources are selected over similar alternatives for which limited coverage is available.

3.3.5 In the case of wrap or sub-accounts, the portfolio's return is comparable to the returns received by institutional clients in the same investment strategy.

INVESTMENT VEHICLES ARE APPROPRIATE FOR THE PORTFOLIO SIZE.

Suggested Procedure

The table below indicates whether commingled accounts (such as mutual funds, exchange traded funds, collective trusts, etc.) or separately managed accounts have a relative advantage with respect to various factors commonly used to determine the most appropriate investment vehicle.

FACTOR	COMMINGLED ACCOUNTS	SEPARATE ACCOUNTS
Ability to manage liquidity		✓
Minimum required investment	✓	
Degree of portfolio diversification	✓	
Ease in managing asset allocation and rebalancing		✓
Availability of data for due diligence	✓	
Fee schedules scaled to portfolio size		✓
Ability to fund the portfolio with assets-in-kind		✓
Avoidance of phantom tax issues (built-in taxable gains)		✓
Ability to manage restricted and low-basis stock issues		✓
Degree of portfolio transparency		✓
Availability of performance reports at the investor level		✓
Degree of regulatory oversight	✓	
Ability to provide direction to the investment manager		✓
Tax deductibility of management fees		✓
Cost		✓
Flexibility to use various active investment strategies		✓

Substantiation

Employee Retirement Income Security Act of 1974 [ERISA]

§404(a)(1)(B); §404(a)(1)(C)

Regulations
29 C.F.R. §2550.404c-1(b)(3)(i)(C)

Case Law
Metzler v. Graham, 112 F.3d 207, 20 E.B.C. 2857 (5th Cir. 1997); *Marshall v. Glass/Metal Ass'n and Glaziers and Glassworkers Pension Plan*, 507 F. Supp. 378 (D.Hawaii 1980); *GIW Industries, Inc. v. Trevor, Stewart, Burton & Jacobsen, Inc.*, 10 E.B.C. 2290 (S.D.Ga. 1989); *aff'd*, 895 F.2d 729 (11th Cir. 1990); *Leigh v. Engle*, 858 F.2d 361, 10 E.B.C. 1041 (7th Cir. 1988), *cert. denied*, 489 U.S. 1078, 109 S.Ct. 1528, 103 L.Ed.2d 833 (1989)

Other
H.R. Report No. 1280, 93rd Congress, 2d Sess. (1974), reprinted in 1974 U.S. Code Cong. & Admin. News 5038 (1974)

Uniform Prudent Investor Act [UPIA]

§2(a); §3; §3 Comments

Uniform Prudent Management of Institutional Funds Act [UPMIFA]

§3(e)

Management of Public Employee Retirement Systems Act [MPERS]

§7(3); §8(a)(1)

A DUE DILIGENCE PROCESS IS FOLLOWED IN SELECTING SERVICE PROVIDERS, INCLUDING THE CUSTODIAN.

Custodial selection is a very important fiduciary function. As with other prudent practices, there are a number of important decisions that need to be managed. The role of the custodian is to: (1) hold securities for safekeeping, (2) report on holdings and transactions, (3) collect interest and dividends, and, if required, (4) effect trades.

At the retail level, the custodian typically is a brokerage firm. Most securities are held in street name, with the assets commingled with those of the brokerage firm. To protect the assets, brokerage firms obtain adequate and appropriate insurance. Most institutional investors choose to use trust companies as custodians and pay an additional custody fee. The primary benefit is that the assets are held in a separate account, and are not commingled with other assets of the institution.

Suggested Procedure

If a client's account is being implemented with a separate account manager, the custodian will likely open a money market fund to serve as the sweep vehicle for dividends and income. The Advisor should inquire as to whether the sweep vehicle is the retail money market fund for the custodian, or the institutional fund. The expense ratio differential between the two can be substantial. If the lower cost alternative is available, ensure that it is implemented.

Many custodians can provide the Investment Advisor information on portfolio performance and tax reporting. Advisors should inquire about the availability even if they are planning to produce the reports in-house. There are numerous ways an error can be made in preparing a performance report, and an additional report, from either a custodian and/or money manager, can make it easier for the Advisor to identify where an error has been made.

Substantiation

Employee Retirement Income Security Act of 1974 [ERISA]

§402(a)(1); §402(b)(2); §404(a)(1)(B)

Other
Interpretive Bulletin 96-1, 29 C.F.R. §2509.96-1; DOL Information Letter, Qualified Plan Services (7/28/98); DOL Information Letter, Service Employee's International Union (2/19/98)

Uniform Prudent Investor Act [UPIA]

§2(a); §7; §7 Comments; §9(a) (1), (2) and (3)

Uniform Prudent Management of Institutional Funds Act [UPMIFA]

§3(b); §3(c); §5(a)

Management of Public Employee Retirement Systems Act [MPERS]

§6(a) and (b)(1) and (2); §7

CRITERIA

3.4.1 A documented due diligence process is applied to select the custodian and all other service providers.

3.4.2 Each custodian has appropriate and adequate insurance to cover each client's portfolio amount.

3.4.3 An appropriate sweep money market fund is selected.

3.4.4 An inquiry has been made as to whether each custodian can facilitate performance reporting and year-end tax statements.

PRACTICE A-4.1

PERIODIC REPORTS COMPARE INVESTMENT PERFORMANCE AGAINST AN APPROPRIATE INDEX, PEER GROUP, AND IPS OBJECTIVES.

CRITERIA

4.1.1 The performance of each investment option is periodically compared against an appropriate index, peer group, and due diligence procedures defined in each client's IPS.

4.1.2 The information that is provided in performance reports is relevant to each client's circumstances.

4.1.3 "Watch list" procedures for underperforming Investment Managers are followed.

4.1.4 Rebalancing procedures are followed.

The Investment Advisor's monitoring function extends beyond a strict examination of performance. By definition, monitoring occurs across all policy and procedural issues previously addressed in this handbook. The ongoing review, analysis, and monitoring of investment decision-makers and/or money managers is just as important as the due diligence implemented during the manager selection process.

In keeping with the duty of prudence, an Investment Advisor must determine the frequency of reviews, taking into account such factors as: (1) prevailing general economic conditions, (2) the size of a client's portfolio, (3) the investment strategies employed, (4) the investment objectives sought, (5) the volatility of the investments selected, and (6) the fiduciary status of the client. The Investment Advisor should monitor every investment option implemented at least quarterly, as required by the facts and circumstances.

The Investment Advisor should establish performance objectives for each investment option, and record the same in the IPS. Investment performance should be evaluated in terms of an appropriate market index, and the relevant peer group. The IPS also should describe the "watch list" procedures to be taken when an investment decision-maker fails to meet the established due diligence criteria and index or benchmark expectations. It should acknowledge that fluctuating rates of return characterize the securities markets, and may cause variations in performance.

The Advisor should evaluate performance from a long-term perspective. The decision to retain or terminate a manager cannot be made by a formula. It is the Investment Advisor's confidence in the money manager's ability to perform in the future that ultimately determines the retention of a money manager.

PERIODIC REPORTS COMPARE INVESTMENT PERFORMANCE AGAINST AN APPROPRIATE INDEX, PEER GROUP, AND IPS OBJECTIVES.

Suggested Procedures:

The monitoring procedures also should include an examination as to whether a client's portfolio requires rebalancing. If it does, the Investment Advisor should inquire of the client as to whether there will be any upcoming contributions and/or disbursements from the portfolio which could be used to more cost effectively rebalance, given tax and transaction cost considerations. Otherwise, rebalancing should be implemented as required by the IPS.

In the absence of any pressing issues of the client, performance reports should be prepared at least quarterly and Advisors should review these reports as they are prepared. Performance reports should be discussed with clients as necessary to keep the portfolio current with the clients' objectives, changes in economic and market conditions, and changes in the outlook for investment positions held. Advisors should insist on holding portfolio performance review sessions with clients no less frequently than annually.

Substantiation

Employee Retirement Income Security Act of 1974 [ERISA]

§3(38); §402(c)(3)

Case Law
Leigh v. Engle, 727 F.2d 113 , 4 E.B.C. 2702(7th Cir. 1984); *Atwood v. Burlington Indus. Equity, Inc.,* 18 E.B.C. 2009 (M.D.N.C. 1994)

Other
Interpretive Bulletin 75-8, 29 C.F.R. §2509.75-8 (FR-17Q); Interpretive Bulletin 94-2, 29 C.F.R. §2509.94-2

Uniform Prudent Investor Act [UPIA]

§2(a); §9(a)(1-3)

Uniform Prudent Management of Institutional Funds Act [UPMIFA]

§3(b); §5(a)

Management of Public Employee Retirement Systems Act [MPERS]

§6(a) and (b)(1 - 3); §6 Comments; §6(d); §8(b)

PERIODIC REVIEWS ARE MADE OF QUALITATIVE AND/OR ORGANIZATIONAL CHANGES OF INVESTMENT DECISION-MAKERS.

The Investment Advisor has a continuing duty to exercise reasonable care, skill, and caution in monitoring the performance of Investment Managers.

The Investment Advisor's review of an Investment Manager must be based on more than recent investment performance results, for all professional money managers will experience periods of poor performance. Advisors also should not be replacing their manager lineup simply because of the reported success of other managers.

In addition to the quantitative reviews of Investment Managers, periodic reviews of the qualitative performance and/or organizational changes to the Managers should be made at reasonable intervals. On a periodic basis (e.g., quarterly) the Advisor should review whether each Investment Manager continues to meet specified objectives. For example:

- The Investment Manager's adherence to the guidelines established by the IPS
- Material changes in the Manager's organization, investment philosophy, and/or personnel
- Any legal or regulatory agency proceedings that may affect the Manager

Suggested Procedure

This handbook is about the practices that define a fiduciary standard of care for Investment Advisors. A companion handbook, *Prudent Practices for Investment Managers*, covers a fiduciary standard of care for Investment Managers. Advisors should be familiar with these practices to help guide reviews of the qualitative and organizational issues that may impact the effectiveness of Investment Managers. Shown below is a list of the practices addressed in the *Prudent Practices for Investment Managers* handbook.

Practice M-1.1 *Senior management demonstrates expertise in their field, and there is a clear succession plan in place.*

Practice M-1.2 *There are clear lines of authority and accountability, and the mission, operations, and resources operate in a coherent manner.*

Practice M-1.3 *The organization has the capacity to service its client base.*

Practice M-1.4 *Administrative operations are structured to provide accurate and timely support services and are conducted in an independent manner.*

Practice M-1.5 *Information systems and technology are sufficient to support administration, trading, and risk management needs.*

Practice M-1.6 *The organization has developed programs to attract, retain, and motivate key employees.*

CRITERIA

4.2.1 Periodic evaluations of the qualitative factors which may impact Investment Managers are performed.

4.2.2 Unsatisfactory news regarding an Investment Manager is documented and acted on in a timely manner.

**PERIODIC REVIEWS ARE MADE OF QUALITATIVE AND/OR
ORGANIZATIONAL CHANGES OF INVESTMENT DECISION-MAKERS.**

Practice M-1.7   *There is a formal structure which supports effective compliance.*

Practice M-2.1   *The organization provides disclosures which demonstrate there are adequate resources to sustain operations.*

Practice M-2.2   *The organization has a defined business strategy which supports their competitive positioning.*

Practice M-2.3   *There is an effective process for allocating and managing both internal and external resources and vendors.*

Practice M-2.4   *There are effective and appropriate external management controls.*

Practice M-2.5   *The organization has a defined process to control its flow of funds and asset variation.*

Practice M-2.6   *Remuneration of the company and compensation of key decision-makers is aligned with client interests.*

Practice M-2.7   *The organization has responsible and ethical reporting, marketing, and sales practices.*

Practice M-2.8   *There is an effective risk-management process to evaluate both the organization's business and investment risk.*

Practice M-3.1   *The asset management team operates in a sustainable, balanced, and cohesive manner.*

Practice M-3.2   *The investment system is defined, focused, and consistently adds value.*

Practice M-3.3   *The investment research process is defined, focused, and documented.*

Practice M-3.4   *The portfolio management process for each distinct strategy is clearly defined, focused, and documented.*

Practice M-3.5   *The trade execution process is defined, focused, and documented.*

Practice M-4.1   *There is a defined process for the attribution and reporting of costs, performance, and risk.*

Practice M-4.2   *All aspects of the investment system are monitored and are consistent with assigned mandates.*

Practice M-4.3   *Control procedures are in place to periodically review policies for best execution, "soft dollars," and proxy voting.*

Practice M-4.4   *There is a process to periodically review the organization's effectiveness in meeting its fiduciary responsibilities.*

Practice A-4.2

Substantiation

Employee Retirement Income Security Act of 1974 [ERISA]

§3(38); §402(c)(3); §404(a)(1)(B)

Regulations
29 C.F.R. §2550.408b-2(d); 29 C.F.R. §2550.408c-2

Other
Interpretive Bulletin 75-8, 29 C.F.R. §2509.75-8; Booklet: A Look at 401(k) Plan Fees, U.S. Department of Labor, Pension and Welfare Benefits Administration

Uniform Prudent Investor Act [UPIA]

§2(a); §7; §9(a)

Uniform Prudent Management of Institutional Funds Act [UPMIFA]

§3(b); §3(c); §5(a)

Management of Public Employee Retirement Systems Act [MPERS]

§6(a) and (b)(1-3); §7(5)

CONTROL PROCEDURES ARE IN PLACE TO PERIODICALLY REVIEW POLICIES FOR BEST EXECUTION, "SOFT DOLLARS," AND PROXY VOTING.

The Investment Advisor has a responsibility to control and account for investment expenses—that the expenses are prudent and are applied in the best interests of the client. When the Advisor is utilizing a separate account manager, managers need to be monitored for:

- *Best execution practices are followed in securities transactions.* The Advisor has a responsibility to seek confirmation that each Investment Manager is seeking best execution in trading the portfolio's securities. In seeking best execution, Investment Managers are required to shop their trades with various brokerage firms, taking into consideration: (1) commission costs, (2) an analysis of the actual execution price of the security, and (3) the quality and reliability (timing) of the trade.

- *"Soft dollars" are expended only for brokerage and research for the benefit of the investment program, and the amount is reasonable in relation to the value of such services.* Soft dollars represent the excess in commission costs: the difference between what a brokerage firm charges for a trade versus the brokerage firm's actual costs. The failure of the Advisor to monitor soft dollars may subject the investment program to expenditures which yield no benefit; itself a fiduciary breach.

- *Proxies are voted in a manner most likely to preserve or enhance the value of the subject stock.* The Advisor can either retain the power to vote the proxies (and maintain documentation of such activity), or instruct an Investment Manager to vote on behalf of the Advisor. If the power to vote proxies is retained, it is imperative that proxies are voted and documented in a timely manner.

Suggested Procedure

One of the easiest ways for an Investment Advisor to monitor a separate account manager's practices for *best execution* and *"soft dollars"* is to watch where the manager is trading the client's account. When the same brokerage firm keeps popping up, additional scrutiny may be required; unless the client has agreed to "directed brokerage," where the client instructs the money manager to trade a percentage of the client's account with a specific broker. This often is the case when a client agrees to a wrap fee arrangement or managed account platform.

CRITERIA

4.3.1 Control procedures are in place to periodically review each separate account manager's policies for best execution.

4.3.2 Control procedures are in place to periodically review each separate account manager's policies for "soft dollars."

4.3.3 Control procedures are in place to periodically review each separate account manager's policies for proxy voting.

Control procedures are in place to periodically review policies for best execution, "soft dollars," and proxy voting.

Substantiation

Employee Retirement Income Security Act of 1974 [ERISA]

§3(38); §402(c)(3); §403(a)(1) and (2); §404(a)(1)(A) and (B)

Case Law
Herman v. NationsBank Trust Co., (Georgia), 126 F.3d 1354, 21 E.B.C. 2061 (11th Cir. 1997), *reh'g denied,* 135 F.3d 1409 (11th Cir.), *cert. denied,* 525 U.S. 816, 19 S.Ct. 54, 142 L.Ed.2d 42 (1998)

Other
Interpretive Bulletin 75-8, 29 C.F.R. §2509.75-8 (FR-17Q); Interpretive Bulletin 94-2, 29 C.F.R. §2509.94-2(1); DOL Prohibited Transaction Exemption 75-1, Interim Exemption, 40 Fed. Reg. 5201 (Feb. 4, 1975); DOL Information Letter, Prescott Asset Management (1/17/92) (fn. 1); DOL Information Letter, Refco, Inc. (2/13/89); ERISA Technical Release 86-1 (May 22, 1986)

Uniform Prudent Investor Act [UPIA]

§2(a); §2(d); §7; §9(a)

Uniform Prudent Management of Institutional Funds Act [UPMIFA]

§3(b); §3(c); §5(a)

Management of Public Employee Retirement Systems Act [MPERS]

§6(2) and (3); §7(5); §8(a)(3)

FEES FOR INVESTMENT MANAGEMENT ARE CONSISTENT WITH AGREEMENTS AND WITH ALL APPLICABLE LAWS.

The Investment Advisor's responsibility in connection with the payment of fees is to determine: (1) whether the fees can be paid from portfolio assets [See also Practice 1.2] and (2) whether the fees are reasonable in light of the services to be provided. [See also Practice 1.5]. Accordingly, the Investment Advisor should ensure all forms of compensation are reasonable for the services rendered.

Suggested Procedure

The Investment Advisor has a duty to control and account for all investment-related expenses, including the expense ratios of mutual funds. If you are using funds or managers with higher than average fees, then you should document the reasons why.

CRITERIA

4.4.1 A summary of all parties being compensated from each client's portfolio has been documented, and the fees are reasonable given the level of services rendered.

4.4.2 The fees paid to each party are periodically examined to determine whether they are consistent with service agreements.

4.4.3 The fees being paid for various services are periodically evaluated for reasonableness.

FEES FOR INVESTMENT MANAGEMENT ARE CONSISTENT WITH AGREEMENTS AND WITH ALL APPLICABLE LAWS.

Substantiation

Employee Retirement Income Security Act of 1974 [ERISA]

§3(14)(B); §404(a)(1)(A), (B) and (D); §406(a)

Regulations
29 C.F.R. §2550.408(b)(2)

Other
Booklet: A Look at 401(k) Plan Fees, U.S. Department of Labor, Pension and Welfare Benefits Administration; DOL Advisory Opinion Letter 2001-01A (1/18/01); DOL Advisory Opinion Letter (7/28/98) 1998; WL 1638072; DOL Advisory Opinion Letter 89-28A (9/25/89) 1989 WL 435076; Interpretive Bulletin 75-8, 29 C.F.R. §2509.75-8 (FR-17Q);

Uniform Prudent Investor Act [UPIA]

§2(a); §7 and Comments; §9 Comments

Uniform Prudent Management of Institutional Funds Act [UPMIFA]

§3(b); §3(c); §5(a)

Management of Public Employee Retirement Systems Act [MPERS]

§7(2) and (5); §7 Comments

"FINDER'S FEES" OR OTHER FORMS OF COMPENSATION THAT MAY HAVE BEEN PAID FOR ASSET PLACEMENT ARE APPROPRIATELY APPLIED, UTILIZED, AND DOCUMENTED.

The Investment Advisor has a duty to account for all dollars spent for investment management services, whether the dollars are paid directly from the account or in the form of "soft dollars" and other fee-sharing arrangements. In addition, the Advisor has the responsibility for identifying those parties that have been compensated from the fees, and applying a reasonableness test to the amount of compensation received by any party.

In the case of an all-inclusive fee (sometimes referred to as a "bundled" or "wrap" fee) investment product, the Investment Advisor should investigate how the various parties associated with each component of the all-inclusive fee are compensated to ensure that no one vendor is receiving unreasonable compensation, and to compare the costs of the same services on an *à la carte* basis.

In the case of defined contribution plans, it is customary to offer investment options that carry fees that often are used to offset the plan's recordkeeping and administrative costs. For a new plan with few assets, such an arrangement is beneficial to the participants.

However, as the assets grow, the fiduciary should periodically determine whether it is more advantageous to pay for the recordkeeping and administrative costs on an *à la carte* basis, switching to mutual funds that have a lower expense ratio, and reducing the overall expenses of the investment program.

Suggested Procedure

Basically, there are four cost components in a *bundled, wrap,* or *all-inclusive fee* investment product. The Investment Advisor should investigate how the various service vendors associated with each component are compensated to ensure that no one vendor is receiving unreasonable compensation, and to compare the costs of the same services on an *à la carte* basis. The four components are:

1. The money manager who is selecting the stocks and bonds for the portfolio.

2. The brokerage firm that is executing the trades.

3. The custodian that is holding and safeguarding the securities.

4. The Investment Advisor, or broker, who is servicing the account.

CRITERIA

4.5.1 All parties compensated from portfolio assets have been identified, along with the amount (or schedule) of their compensation.

4.5.2 Compensation paid from portfolio assets has been determined to be fair and reasonable for the services rendered.

"FINDER'S FEES" OR OTHER FORMS OF COMPENSATION THAT MAY HAVE BEEN PAID FOR ASSET PLACEMENT ARE APPROPRIATELY APPLIED, UTILIZED, AND DOCUMENTED.

Unbundling Fees and Expenses

"Bundled fees" should be broken down into four categories so that a proper evaluation can be made – various costs can be obscured or moved to create apparent savings.

Substantiation

Employee Retirement Income Security Act of 1974 [ERISA]

§404(a)(1)(A) and (B);§406(a)(1); §406(b)(1); §406(b)(3)

Case Law
Brock v. Robbins, 830 F.2d 640, 8 E.B.C. 2489 (7th Cir. 1987)

Other
DOL Advisory Opinion Letter 97-15A; DOL Advisory Opinion Letter 97-16A (5/22/97)

Uniform Prudent Investor Act [UPIA]

§2(a); §7; §7 Comments

Case Law
Matter of Derek W. Bryant, 188 Misc. 2d 462, 729 NYS 2d 309 (6/21/01)

Other
McKinneys EPTL11-2.3(d)

Uniform Prudent Management of Institutional Funds Act [UPMIFA]

§3(b); §3(c)

Management of Public Employee Retirement Systems Act [MPERS]

§6(b)(2) and (3); §7(2) and (5)

THERE IS A PROCESS TO PERIODICALLY REVIEW THE ORGANIZATION'S EFFECTIVENESS IN MEETING ITS FIDUCIARY RESPONSIBILITIES.

Fiduciary duties generally are presented as distinct obligations substantiated through law and regulation. Many of the duties are accompanied by documentation and review obligations. As a practical matter, a comprehensive framework is needed to ensure that all applicable fiduciary practices are fully and effectively addressed on an ongoing basis. A planned approach to conduct periodic reviews provides such a framework.

Given that internal and external reviews and assessments are well-recognized tools to evaluate risks and ensure the effectiveness of policies and procedures, further weight is added to the need to establish a formal overall review process (as is provided by an assessment program).

Finally, it is important to recognize that the trend in law and regulation is towards greater formality in: (1) policies and procedures and (2) processes to ensure that the policies and procedures are effective.

Suggested Procedure

There are three levels of fiduciary reviews or assessments. These levels are analogous to the levels used in auditing for conformity to accounting and ISO standards.

Level 1 is a self-assessment. This is analogous to an internal audit. Every fiduciary organization (including the Advisor's firm) should periodically conduct a formal review of its own policies, procedures and activities to determine the extent to which they fulfill the practices presented in this handbook.

Level 2 is a consultant's (or related party) assessment. A Level 2 assessment is conducted by an outside, independent analyst engaged to systematically evaluate a fiduciary organization's fiduciary practices. The analyst will also generally provide assistance to the assessed entity in correcting any shortfalls. An Advisor with training and experience in the areas of fiduciary responsibility and fiduciary assessments may choose to provide Level 2 assessments for other fiduciary organizations.

Level 3 is an independent assessment. Analysts who conduct independent assessments must not be affiliated or have other business relationships with the assessed entity. Like independent financial audits, Level 3 fiduciary assessments may be conducted to demonstrate that an organization has undergone a rigorous and objective process to determine its conformity to set standards.

Under the Pension Protection Act of 2006 (PPA), the practices of plan sponsors and fiduciary advisers who are party to eligible investment advice arrangements (EIAA) will be examined as part of the required annual independent audit of the EIAA. Advisors who provide advisory services to ERISA plans and who serve as fiduciary advisers should take special note of this audit provision in the PPA.

CRITERIA

4.6.1 Operational effectiveness is periodically reviewed to foster continued improvement.

4.6.2 Assessments are conducted at planned intervals to determine whether (a) appropriate policies and procedures are in place to address all fiduciary obligations, and (b) such policies and procedures are effectively implemented and maintained, and (c) the IPS is up-to-date.

4.6.3 Assessments are documented, conducted in a manner that ensures objectivity and impartiality, and results are reviewed for reasonableness.

THERE IS A PROCESS TO PERIODICALLY REVIEW THE ORGANIZATION'S EFFECTIVENESS IN MEETING ITS FIDUCIARY RESPONSIBILITIES.

Substantiation

Employee Retirement Income Security Act of 1974 [ERISA]

§404(a)(1)(B)

Case Law
Chao v. Chacon, Case No. 1:04 CV 35000 (N.D. Ohio 2005); *Fink v. National Savings & Trust Co.*, 772 F.2d 951, 957 (D.C. Cir. 1985); *Liss v. Smith*, 991 F.Supp. 278, 299-300 (S.D.N.Y.,1998).

Other
Department of Labor Employee Benefits Security Administration, "Meeting Your Fiduciary Responsibilities" (May 2004); 29 C.F.R. 2509.75-8; 29 C.F.R. 2509.94-2; 17 C.F.R. § 275.206(4)-7; DOL Field Assistance Bulletin 2007-01.

Uniform Prudent Investor Act [UPIA]

§2(a); §2(d)

Uniform Management of Public Employee Retirement Systems Act [MPERS]

§8(b); §7

As noted on page 7 of this Prudent Practices handbook, the approach used to structure the practices is modeled after that used by the International Organization for Standardization (ISO). Recently, the financial services community has begun to recognize the value of certification of conformity to standards. There is now an ISO standard for financial planning (ISO 22222) and investment performance reporting practices can be certified to Global Investment Performance Standards (GIPS). In 2006, the Center for Fiduciary Excellence (CEFEX) was formed to certify conformity with the practices covered in the Prudent Practices for Investment Fiduciaries handbook series. Fi360 is a founding member of CEFEX.

The Practices identified in this handbook prescribe a process that strives for excellence in the management of investment decisions. Yet they remain flexible enough to account for the continual changes in the investment world. Once familiar with the Practices, the Investment Advisor should understand that no new investment product or technique is good or bad per se; nor will it be valuable simply because it worked for other Advisors. Furthermore, the Practices will help the Investment Advisor understand which new investment strategies, products, and techniques fit into their operations, and which do not.

The intelligent and prudent management of investment decisions requires the Advisor to maintain a rational, disciplined investment program. The mind-boggling array of investment choices, coupled with market noise from stock markets around the world, understandably can result in financial paralysis from information overload. Investment Advisors clearly need a framework for managing investment decisions that allows them to consider developing investment trends, and to thoughtfully navigate the possibilities.

The Board of Directors for the Foundation for Fiduciary Studies

The Staff of Fi360

The AICPA's Personal Financial Planning Executive Committee

Investment Policy Statement

This Investment Policy Statement (IPS) has been prepared by fi360 and has not been reviewed, nor is it endorsed, by the AICPA. It is intended to serve as an example of the type of information that would be included in a comprehensive IPS. Investment Advisors are advised to have legal counsel review their IPS before it is approved.

High Net Worth Individual / Family Wealth

(Client)

Approved on (Date)

This investment policy statement should be reviewed and updated at least annually. Any change to this policy should be communicated in writing on a timely basis to all interested parties.

Executive Summary

Type of Client: Taxable, Individual

Current Assets: $650,000

Time Horizon: Greater than 5 years

Modeled Return: 8.0%

Modeled Loss: -9.4% (Probability level of 5%)

Asset Allocation:

	Lower Limit	Strategic Allocation	Upper Limit
Domestic Large-Cap Equity			
Blend	5%	10%	15%
Growth	5	10	15
Value	5	10	15
Mid-Cap Equity	5	10	15
Small-Cap Equity	5	10	15
International Equity	5	10	15
Intermediate-term Fixed Income	30	35	40
Cash Equivalent	0	5	10

Purpose

The purpose of this Investment Policy Statement (IPS) is to assist the Client and Investment Advisor (Advisor) in effectively supervising, monitoring, and evaluating the investment of the Client's Portfolio (Portfolio). The Client's investment program is defined in the various sections of the IPS by:

1. Stating in a written document the Client's attitudes, expectations, objectives, and guidelines for the investment of all assets.

2. Setting forth an investment structure for managing the Client's Portfolio. This structure includes various asset classes, investment management styles, asset allocations, and acceptable ranges that, in total, are expected to produce an appropriate level of overall diversification and total investment return over the investment time horizon.

3. Encouraging effective communications between the Client and the Advisor.

4. Establishing formal criteria to select, monitor, evaluate, and compare the performance of money managers on a regular basis.

5. Complying with all applicable fiduciary, prudence, and due diligence requirements experienced investment professionals would utilize; and with all applicable laws, rules, and regulations from various local, state, federal, and international political entities that may impact the Client's assets.

Background

This IPS has been prepared for John and Mary HNW Client (Client), a taxable entity. The assets covered by this IPS currently total approximately $650,000 in market value, but the Client's net worth is estimated to be $1,225,000. Assets not covered by this IPS include:

(1) Corporate-sponsored defined contribution programs, where both the husband and wife participate (combined, valued at $350,000); and

(2) A vacation condo valued at $225,000.

Statement of Objectives

This IPS describes the prudent investment process the Advisor deems appropriate for the Client's situation. The Client desires to maximize returns within prudent levels of risk, and to meet the following stated investment objectives:

> Advisor lists investment objectives:
>
> 1. Retire with sufficient assets to support a lifestyle of _____.
>
> 2. Provide college tuition to grandchildren, etc.

Time Horizon

The investment guidelines are based upon an investment horizon of greater than five years; therefore, interim fluctuations should be viewed with appropriate perspective. Short-term liquidity requirements are anticipated to be minimal.

Risk Tolerances

The Client recognizes and acknowledges some risk must be assumed in order to achieve long-term investment objectives, and there are uncertainties and complexities associated with contemporary investment markets.

In establishing the risk tolerances for this IPS, the Client's ability to withstand short- and intermediate- term variability was considered. The Client's prospects for the future, current financial condition, and several other factors suggest collectively some interim fluctuations in market value and rates of return may be tolerated in order to achieve the longer-term objectives.

Expected Return

In general, the Client would like the assets to earn at least a targeted return of 8.0%. It is understood that an average return of 8.0% will require superior manager performance to: (1) retain principal value; and, (2) purchasing power. Furthermore, the objective is to earn a long-term rate of return at least 5.5% greater than the rate of inflation as measured by the Consumer Price Index (CPI).

Asset Class Preferences

The Client understands long-term investment performance, in large part, is primarily a function of asset class mix. The Client has reviewed the long-term performance characteristics of the broad asset classes, focusing on balancing the risks and rewards.

History shows that while interest-generating investments such as bond portfolios have the advantage of relative stability of principal value, they provide little opportunity for real long-term capital growth due to their susceptibility to inflation. On the other hand, equity investments, such as common stocks, clearly have a significantly higher expected return, but have the disadvantage of much greater year-by-year variability of return. From an investment decision-making point of view, this year-by-year variability may be worth accepting, provided the time horizon for the equity portion of the portfolio is sufficiently long (five years or greater).

The following eight asset classes were selected and ranked in ascending order of "risk" (least to most).

> Money Market (MM)
> Intermediate Bond (IB)
> Large Cap Value (LCV)
> Large Cap Blend (LCB)
> Large Cap Growth (LCG)
> Mid Cap Blend (MCB)
> Small Cap Blend (SCB)
> International Equity (IE)

The Client has considered the following asset classes for inclusion in the asset mix, but has decided to exclude these asset classes at the present time:

> Global Fixed Income
> Real Estate

Rebalancing of Strategic Allocation

The percentage allocation to each asset class may vary as much as plus or minus 5% depending upon market conditions. When necessary and/or available, cash inflows/outflows will be deployed in a manner consistent with the strategic asset allocation of the Portfolio. If there are no cash flows, the allocation of the Portfolio will be reviewed quarterly.

If the Advisor judges cash flows to be insufficient to bring the Portfolio within the strategic allocation ranges, the Client shall decide whether to effect transactions to bring the strategic allocation within the threshold ranges (**Strategic Allocation**).

Duties and Responsibilities

Investment Advisor

The Client has retained an objective, third-party Advisor to assist the Client in managing the investments. The Advisor will be responsible for guiding the Client through a disciplined and rigorous investment process. As a fiduciary to the Client, the primary responsibilities of the Advisor are:

1. Prepare and maintain this investment policy statement.

2. Provide sufficient asset classes with different and distinct risk/return profiles so that the Client can prudently diversify the Portfolio.

3. Prudently select investment options.

4. Control and account for all investment expenses.

5. Monitor and supervise all service vendors and investment options.

6. Avoid prohibited transactions and conflicts of interest.

Investment Managers

As distinguished from the Advisor, who is responsible for *managing* the investment process, investment managers are responsible for *making* investment decisions (security selection and price decisions). The specific duties and responsibilities of each investment manager are:

1. Manage the assets under their supervision in accordance with the guidelines and objectives outlined in their respective Service Agreements, Prospectus, or Trust Agreement.

2. Exercise full investment discretion with regard to buying, managing, and selling assets held in the portfolios.

3. If managing a separate account (as opposed to a mutual fund or a commingled account), seek approval from the Client prior to purchasing and/or implementing the following securities and transactions:

   - Letter stock and other unregistered securities; commodities and other commodity contracts; and short sales or margin transactions.

   - Securities lending; pledging or hypothecating securities.

   - Investments in the equity securities of any company with a record of less than three years of continuous operation, including the operation of any predecessor.

   - Investments for the purpose of exercising control of management.

4. Vote promptly all proxies and related actions in a manner consistent with the long-term interests and objectives of the Portfolio as described in this IPS. Each investment manager shall keep detailed records of the voting of proxies and related actions and will comply with all applicable regulatory obligations.

5. Communicate to the Client all significant changes pertaining to the fund it manages or the firm itself. Changes in ownership, organizational structure, financial condition, and professional staff are examples of changes to the firm of interest to the Client.

6. Effect all transactions for the Portfolio subject "to best price and execution." If a manager utilizes brokerage from the Portfolio assets to effect "soft dollar" transactions, detailed records will be kept and communicated to the Client.

7. Use the same care, skill, prudence, and due diligence under the circumstances then prevailing that experienced investment professionals—acting in a like capacity and fully familiar with such matters —would use in like activities for like Portfolios with like aims in accordance and compliance with the Uniform Prudent Investor Act and all applicable laws, rules, and regulations.

8. If managing a separate account (as opposed to a mutual fund or a commingled account), acknowledge co-fiduciary responsibility by signing and returning a copy of this IPS.

Custodian

Custodians are responsible for the safekeeping of the Portfolio's assets. The specific duties and responsibilities of the custodian are:

1. Maintain separate accounts by legal registration.

2. Value the holdings.

3. Collect all income and dividends owed to the Portfolio.

4. Settle all transactions (buy-sell orders) initiated by the Investment Manager.

5. Provide monthly reports that detail transactions, cash flows, securities held and their current value, and change in value of each security and the overall portfolio since the previous report.

Investment Manager Selection

A suggested minimum due diligence process would include the following:

1. *Regulatory oversight:* Each investment option should be managed by: (a) a bank, (b) an insurance company, (c) a registered investment company (mutual fund), or (d) a registered investment adviser.

2. *Minimum track record:* Each investment option should have at least three years of history so that performance statistics can be properly calculated.

3. *Stability of the organization:* The same portfolio management team should be in place for at least two years.

4. *Assets in the product:* Each investment option should have at least $75 million under management (for mutual funds - can include assets in related share classes).

5. *Holdings consistent with style:* At least 80% of the underlying securities should be consistent with the broad asset class.

6. *Correlation to style or peer group:* Each investment option should be highly correlated to the asset class being implemented.

7. *Expense ratios/fees:* Fees should not be in the bottom quartile (most expensive) of the peer group.

8. *Performance relative to assumed risk:* The investment option's risk-adjusted performance (Alpha and/or Sharpe Ratio) should be evaluated against the peer group median manager's risk-adjusted performance.

9. *Performance relative to peer group:* Each investment option's performance should be evaluated against the peer group's median manager return, for 1-, 3- and 5-year cumulative periods.

Control Procedures

Performance Objectives

The Client acknowledges fluctuating rates of return characterize the securities markets, particularly during short-term time periods. Recognizing that short-term fluctuations may cause variations in performance, the Advisor intends to evaluate manager performance from a long-term perspective.

The Client is aware the ongoing review and analysis of the investment managers is just as important as the due diligence implemented during the manager selection process. The performance of the investment managers will be monitored on an ongoing basis and it is at the Client's discretion to take corrective action by replacing a manager if they deem it appropriate at any time.

On a timely basis, but not less than quarterly, the Advisor will meet with the Client to review whether each manager continues to conform to the search criteria outlined in the previous section; specifically:

1. The manager's adherence to the Portfolio's investment guidelines;

2. Material changes in the manager's organization, investment philosophy, and/or personnel; and,

3. Any legal, SEC, and/or other regulatory agency proceedings affecting the manager.

The Advisor has determined that it is in the best interest of the Client that performance objectives be established for each investment manager. Manager performance will be evaluated in terms of an appropriate market index (e.g., the S&P 500 stock index for large-cap domestic equity manager) and the relevant peer group (e.g., the large-cap growth mutual fund universe for a large-cap growth mutual fund).

Asset Class	Index	Peer Group
Large-Cap Equity		
Blend	S&P 500	Large-Cap Blend
Growth	Russell 200 Growth	Large-Cap Growth
Value	Russell 200 Value	Large-Cap Value
Mid-Cap Equity	S&P 400	Mid-Cap Blend
Small-Cap Equity	Russell 2000	Small-Cap Blend
International Equity	MSCI EAFE	Foreign Stock
Fixed Income		
Intermediate-term Bond	Lehman Brothers Gov't/ Credit Intermediate	Intermediate-term Bond
Money Market	90-day T-Bills	Money Market Database

A manager may be placed on a "Watchlist" and a thorough *review* and *analysis* of the investment manager may be conducted, when:

1. A manager performs below median for their peer group over a 1-, 3-, and/or 5-year cumulative period.

2. A manager's 3-year risk adjusted return (Alpha and/or Sharpe) falls below the peer group's median risk adjusted return.

3. There is a change in the professionals managing the portfolio.

4. There is a significant decrease in the product's assets.

5. There is an indication the manager is deviating from his/her stated style and/or strategy.

6. There is an increase in the product's fees and expenses.

7. Any extraordinary event occurs that may interfere with the manager's ability to fulfill their role in the future.

A manager evaluation may include the following steps:

1. A letter to the manager asking for an analysis of their underperformance.

2. An analysis of recent transactions, holdings, and portfolio characteristics to determine the cause for underperformance or to check for a change in style.

3. A meeting with the manager, which may be conducted on-site, to gain insight into organizational changes and any changes in strategy or discipline.

The decision to retain or terminate a manager cannot be made by a formula. It is the Client's confidence in the manager's ability to perform in the future that ultimately determines the retention of a manager.

Measuring Costs

The Advisor will review with the Client, at least annually, all costs associated with the management of the Portfolio's investment program, including:

1. Expense ratios of each investment option against the appropriate peer group.

2. Custody fees: The holding of the assets, collection of the income, and disbursement of payments.

3. Whether the manager is demonstrating attention to "best execution" in trading securities.

Investment Policy Review

The Advisor will review this IPS with the Client at least annually to determine whether stated investment objectives are still relevant, and the continued feasibility of achieving the same. It is not expected that the IPS will change frequently. In particular, short-term changes in the financial markets should not require adjustments to the IPS.

Prepared: Approved:

_____   _____

Advisor   Client

Date _____   Date _____

GLOSSARY OF TERMS

This glossary was compiled from the following sources:

Eugene B. Burroughs, CFA, *Investment Terminology* (Revised Edition), International Foundation of Employee Benefit Plans, Inc., 1993.

John Downes and Jordan Elliot Goodman, *Dictionary of Finance and Investment Terms* (Third Edition), Barron's Educational Series, Inc., 1991.

John W. Guy, *How to Invest Someone Else's Money*, Irwin Professional Publishing, Burr Ridge, Illinois, 1994.

Donald B. Trone, William R. Allbright, and Philip R. Taylor, *The Management of Investment Decisions*, Irwin Professional Publishing, Burr Ridge, Illinois, 1995.

Donald B. Trone, William R. Allbright, and Philip R. Taylor, *Procedural Prudence for Fiduciaries*, self-published, 1997.

AIF® (Accredited Investment Fiduciary®) – Professional designation signifying knowledge and competency in fiduciary responsibility. It is designed for those who wish to adopt the global fiduciary standard of excellence. The designation can be earned by successful completion of a Web-based program or a 2-day classroom program.

AIFA® (Accredited Investment Fiduciary Analyst™) – Professional designation for those who wish to conduct ISO-like assessments of a global fiduciary standard of excellence. Certification procedures have been developed for the evaluation of Investment Advisors, Investment Managers, and Investment Stewards. The AIFA can be earned by successfully obtaining the AIF designation, completing a 3-day AIFA program, and meeting certain other prerequisites and requirements.

Alpha – This statistic measures a portfolio's return in excess of the market return adjusted for risk. It is a measure of the Manager's contribution to performance with reference to security selection. A positive alpha indicates that a portfolio was positively rewarded for the residual risk, which was taken for that level of market exposure.

Analyst – A person approved by CEFEX or fi360 to conduct an assessment for *Certification*.

Assessment – The process of determining whether a fiduciary conforms with defined *Practices* and *Criteria*.

Asset Allocation – The process of determining the optimal allocation of a fund's portfolio among broad asset classes.

Audit – (*verb*) The process of gathering, displaying, and verifying information and data that will be used to assess whether there is conformance with a *Standard*.

Basis Point – One hundredth of a percent (100 Basis Points = 1%).

GLOSSARY OF TERMS

Best Execution – Formally defined as the difference between the execution price (the price at which a security is actually bought or sold) and the "fair market price," which involves calculating opportunity costs by examining the security price immediately after the trade is placed. Best execution occurs when the trade involves no lost opportunity cost; for example, when there is no increase in the price of a security shortly after it is sold.

Cash Sweep Accounts – A money market fund into which all new contributions, stock dividend income, and bond interest income is placed ("swept") for a certain period of time. At regular intervals, or when rebalancing is necessary, this cash is invested in assets in line with the asset allocation stipulated in the IPS.

CEFEX, Centre for Fiduciary Excellence – An independent global assessment and certification organization. CEFEX works closely with investment fiduciaries and industry experts to provide comprehensive assessment programs to improve risk management for institutional and retail investors. CEFEX certification helps determine trustworthiness of investment fiduciaries.

CFA Institute (formerly AIMR) Performance Presentation Standards – These standards, effective January 1, 1993, are designed to promote full disclosure and fair representation in the reporting of investment results in order to provide uniformity in comparing Manager results. These standards include ethical principles, and apply to all organizations serving investment management functions. Compliance is verified at two levels: Level 1 and Level 2. (Level 2 is a more comprehensive verification process).

Commingled Fund – An investment fund that is similar to a mutual fund in that investors purchase and redeem units that represent ownership in a pool of securities. Commingled funds usually are offered through a bank-administered plan allowing for broader and more efficient investing.

Commission Recapture – An agreement by which a plan Fiduciary earns credits based upon the amount of brokerage commissions paid. These credits can be used for services that will benefit the plan such as consulting services, custodian fees, or hardware and software expenses.

Correlation Coefficient – Correlation measures the degree to which two variables are associated. Correlation is a commonly used tool for constructing a well-diversified portfolio. Traditionally, equities and fixed-income asset returns have not moved closely together. The asset returns are not strongly correlated. A balanced fund with equities and fixed-income assets represents a diversified portfolio that attempts to take advantage of the low correlation between the two asset classes.

Criteria – The details of a defined *Practice* and serve as the basis for a Global Standard of Excellence.

Directed Brokerage – Circumstances in which a board of trustees or other fiduciary requests that the Investment Manager direct trades to a particular broker so that the commissions generated can be used for specific services \or resources. See **"Soft Dollars."**

Economically-Targeted Investment (ETI) – Investments where the goal is to target a certain economic activity, sector, or area in order to produce corollary benefits in addition to the main objective of earning a competitive risk-adjusted rate of return.

GLOSSARY OF TERMS

ERISA – The Employee Retirement Income Security Act is a 1974 U.S. law governing the operation of most private pension and benefit plans. The law eased pension eligibility rules, set up the Pension Benefit Guaranty Corporation, and established guidelines for the management of pension funds.

Fi360 – An organization that promotes a culture of fiduciary responsibility and improves the decision making processes of investment fiduciaries. With defined practices as a foundation, offers training, tools, and resources for investment fiduciaries.

Fiduciary – From the Latin word *fiducia*, meaning "trust." Someone who stands in a special relation of trust, confidence, and/or legal responsibility. A fiduciary is held to a standard of conduct and trust above that of a stranger or of a casual business person due to the superior knowledge and/or training of the fiduciary.

Fiduciary Adviser – A term introduced under the 2006 Pension Protection Act; an Investment Advisor selected by an ERISA plan sponsor to provide specific investment advice to plan participants.

Fiduciary Excellence – Is a function of how well *Investment Stewards, Investment Advisors,* and *Investment Managers* follow defined fiduciary *Practices* and *Criteria.*

Investment Advisor – A professional fiduciary who is responsible for managing comprehensive and continuous investment decisions (including wealth managers, financial advisors, trust officers, financial consultants, investment consultants, and financial planners).

Investment Manager – A professionals who has discretion to select specific securities for separate accounts, mutual funds, commingled trusts, and unit trusts.

Investment Steward – A person who has the legal responsibility for managing investment decisions (trustees and investment committee members).

Liquidity Risk – The risk that there will be insufficient cash to meet the fund's disbursement and expense requirements.

Money Markets – Financial markets in which financial assets with a maturity of less than one year are traded. Money market funds also refer to open-end mutual funds that invest in low-risk, highly liquid, short-term financial instruments and whose net asset value is kept stable at $1 per share. The average portfolio maturity is 30 to 60 days.

Practice – (*noun*) The details of a prudent process.

Proxy Voting – A written authorization given by a shareholder to someone else to vote his or her shares at a stockholders annual or special meeting called to elect directors or for some other corporate purpose.

Rater – A person approved by Cefex to conduct a *Rating.*

Rating – The process of determining whether a fiduciary exceeds, and to what degree it exceeds, a *Standard.*

Real Estate Investment Trust (REIT) – An investment fund whose objective is to hold real estate-related assets; either through mortgages, construction and development loans, or equity interests.

Risk-Adjusted Return – The return on an asset, or portfolio, modified to explicitly account for the risk of the asset or portfolio.

Risk-Free Rate of Return – The return on 90-day U.S. Treasury Bills. This is used as a proxy for no risk due to its zero default risk issuance, minimal "interest rate" risk and high marketability. The term is really a misnomer since nothing is free of risk. It is utilized since certain economic models require a "risk-free" point of departure. See **Sharpe Ratio**.

R-squared (R^2 or R2) – Formally called the coefficient of determination, this measures the overall strength or "explanatory power" of a statistical relationship. In general, a higher R2 means a stronger statistical relationship between the variables that have been estimated, and therefore more confidence in using the estimation for decision-making. Primarily used to determine the appropriateness of a given index in evaluating a Manager's performance.

Safe Harbor Rules – A series of guidelines which, when in full compliance, may limit a fiduciary's liabilities.

Sharpe Ratio – This statistic is a commonly used measure of risk-adjusted return. It is calculated by subtracting the Risk-Free Return (usually 3-Month U.S. Treasury Bill) from the portfolio return and dividing the resulting "excess return" by the portfolio's total risk level (standard deviation). The result is a measure of return gained per unit of total risk taken. The Sharpe Ratio can be used to compare the relative performance of Managers. If two managers have the same level of risk but different levels of excess return, the manager with the higher Sharpe Ratio would be preferable. The Sharpe Ratio is most helpful when comparing managers with both different returns and different levels of risk. In this case, the Sharpe Ratio provides a per-unit measure of the two managers that enables a comparison.

Socially-Targeted Investment or Socially Responsible Investment (SRI) – An investment that is undertaken based upon social, rather than purely financial, guidelines. See also **Economically-Targeted Investment**.

Soft Dollars – The portion of a commission's expense for trading a security which is in excess of the actual cost of executing the trade by the broker-dealer.

Standard of Excellence – The *Practices* and *Criteria* which detail a prudent process and the attributes of a trustworthy fiduciary.

Components of a Standard

Standard Deviation – A statistical measure of portfolio risk. It reflects the average deviation of the observations from their sample mean. Standard deviation is used as an estimate of risk since it measures how wide the range of returns typically is. The wider the typical range of returns, the higher the standard deviation of returns, and the higher the portfolio risk. If returns were normally distributed (i.e., has a bell-shaped curve distribution) then approximately two-thirds of the returns would occur within plus or minus one standard deviation from the sample mean.

Strategic Asset Allocation – Rebalancing back to the normal mix at specified time intervals (quarterly) or when established tolerance bands are violated (±5%).

Tactical Asset Allocation – The "first cousin" to **Market Timing** because it uses certain "indicators" to make adjustments in the proportions of portfolio invested in three asset classes – stocks, bonds, and cash.

Trading Costs – Behind investment management fees, trading accounts for the second highest cost of plan administration. Trading costs are usually quoted in cents per share. As of the date of this publication, median institutional trading costs range from 5 to 7 cents per share.

90-Day U.S. Treasury Bill – The 90-Day T-Bill provides a measure of riskless return. The rate of return is the average interest rate available in the beginning of each month for a T-Bill maturing in 90 days. In Europe, the London Inter-Bank Offered Rate (LIBOR) is also used as a risk-free benchmark.

Variance – A statistical measure that indicates the spread of values within a set of outcomes around a calculated average. For example, the range of daily prices for a stock will have a variance over a time period that reflects the amount that the stock price varies from the average, or mean, price of the stock over the time period. Variance is useful as a risk statistic because it gives an indication of how much the value of the portfolio might fluctuate up or down from the average value over a given time.